THE

JAPANESE

THE

JAPANESE

People of the Three Treasures

ROBERT NEWMAN

drawings by Mamoru Funai

ATHENEUM 1966 NEW YORK

For JOLIE *and* TOMMY
and all their contemporaries.

Acknowledgments

For permission to use quotations, I gratefully make the following acknowledgments:

To Routledge and Kegan Paul, Ltd. for the letter describing a Portuguese arquebus from James Murdoch's *A History of Japan,* copyright by Kegan Paul, London, 1926.

To the Bollingen Foundation for the description of the spirit of *cha-no-yu* from *Zen and Japanese Culture* by Daisetz Suzuki, published for the Bollingen Foundation by Pantheon Books, Inc., New York, copyright 1959.

To Appleton-Century-Crofts, Inc. for the letter from Saicho to his disciple from *Japan: A Short Cultural History* by G. B. Sansom, Revised Edition, copyright 1943.

To Houghton Mifflin Company for the passage from *The Tale of Genji,* translated by Arthur Waley, copyright 1925.

To Kobusai Bunka Shinkokai for excerpts from *The Beginner's Book of Bushido,* translated by A. L. Sadler, copyright 1941.

To the Asiatic Society of Japan for the Book of Swords passage from the *Heike Monogatori,* translated by A. L. Sadler and published in the "Transactions of the Asiatic Society of Japan," copyright 1920.

I would like to take this opportunity to thank Mr. Eugene Langston of the Japan Society for answering many questions for me while this book was in preparation and for reading the manuscript when it was finished and making many valuable comments on it.

I would also like to thank Miss Sylvia Hilton and Miss Helen Ruskell of the New York Society Library for their help, patience and understanding during the time that the book was in work.

My most profound thanks, however, must go to my friend, Mr. Jay Williams, who first introduced me to things Japanese and particularly the Japanese sword. It was he who urged me to write this book and not only lent me much material from his own extensive library of Orientalia, but also read the manuscript and made many suggestions that were extremely helpful.

Contents

CHINA

KOREA

SEA OF

20 miles
Lake Biwa and environs

LAKE BIWA

Kyoto • • Azuchi
• Momoyama

Osaka •
• • Nara
Sakai • YAMATO

TSUSHIMA

IKISHIMA HAKATA BAY

Hirado

Dazaifu

Bungo

Shimabara

Satsuma

KYUSHU

Izumo

Dannoura

Ichinotani

Ako

LAKE BIWA

Kyoto
Osaka

Sakai

SHIKOKU

TANEGASHIMA

The Main Islands of

JAPAN

SCALE OF MILES

0   50   100   200

I

*The Gods
and the
Treasures*

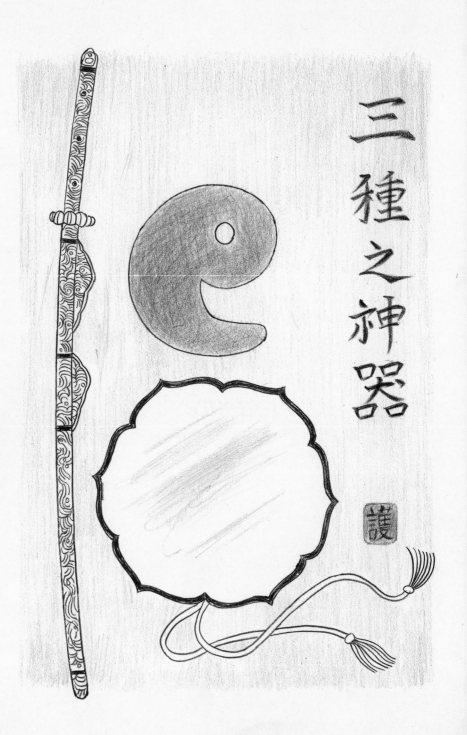

三種之神器

1

The Three Treasures

Before the land was or the people, there were the gods.

Standing on the arch of the rainbow, Izanagi dipped his spear into the flux below and let the drops fall on the face of the waters where they became solid and took the form of islands, some small and some large. Looking down and finding that the land he had created was fair, Izanagi and his sister, Izanami, descended from heaven and for a time lived on this favored portion of the earth which was Japan.

Later, after going to the Land of the Dead, Izanagi created all the other gods, among whom were Amaterasu or Shining in Heaven, and Susanowo, Impetuous Male. Amaterasu was the sun-goddess—lovely, gentle and life-giving—and she lived on high, while Susanowo roared through the middle air between heaven and earth, a destroying storm-god.

Coming one day to visit Amaterasu in heaven, Susanowo's behavior was even more disgraceful than usual for he ruined her garden and broke the dykes between her rice fields.

Outraged, Amaterasu hid herself in a cave, refusing to leave it, and darkness came on the world: eternal darkness that could mean the end of all living things. All the myriad *kami* or local gods of mountains, lakes, and forests, assembled at the mouth of the cave and begged Amaterasu to return to them. When she refused, they decorated a magic mirror with curved, sacred jewels and set it up in front of the cave. Then one of the goddesses did a comic dance which made all the other kami laugh. Intrigued, Amaterasu peeped out of the cave to see what they were laughing at. Catching sight of herself in the mirror, she came out of the cave to see who this glorious creature was, and one of the gods rolled a huge stone in front of it to keep her from returning to it.

For his sins, Susanowo was exiled from heaven to the Land of Darkness. He did not go there at once, however, but lived for a time at Izumo, on the northern coast of Japan facing the Korean peninsula.

Walking abroad one day, looking for adventure, Susanowo came upon an old man and woman who were weeping because their daughter had just been condemned to be eaten by the Dragon of Koshi, an enormous monster with eight heads and eight tails, which had been ravaging the district for many years. Susanowo had eight tubs of *sake* or rice wine brewed and placed in the dragon's path. When the dragon had lapped up the sake and fallen into a drunken stupor, Susanowo killed it and found in one of his tails a marvelous sword.

To make amends for his earlier misdeeds, Susanowo gave the sword to Amaterasu, who named it the Sword of the Clustering Clouds of Heaven. Susanowo married the girl he had saved from the dragon and they had many children, but none were thought worthy of ruling the land created by Izanagi. Instead, Amaterasu sent down her grandson, Ninigi, to be its first emperor. As a token of his divine mission, she gave him three treasures: the mirror that had lured her from the cave; one of the curved, sacred jewels which had decorated it; and the sword that Susanowo had found in the dragon's tail. With these, she declared, he should rule the fertile rice land of Japan, and his dynasty should prosper and endure forever.

Years later, the sword came into the possession of Prince Yamato Dake or the Bravest of the Yamato, one of the descendants of Ninigi, and it acquired a new name. For one day Yamato Dake was trapped upon a moor by enemies who tried to destroy him by setting fire to the long dry grass. But the magic sword leaped from its sheath and cut such a wide swathe around him that the fire could not reach him. From that time on it was known as *Kusanagi* or Grass Cutter.

So far as we know, Amaterasu kept her promise to Ninigi. For the ancestors of the present emperor of Japan go back to the mists of antiquity, long before there were written records; the imperial family is probably the oldest royal line in the world. What is more, the Three Treasures—the Mirror, the Jewel, and the Sword—still exist today: the Mirror at Ise, the most sacred shrine in Japan; the Sword at the Atsuta shrine near Nagoya; and the Jewel at the imperial palace in Tokyo.

And while, despite the myths, the Three Treasures are not of celestial origin—and may even have been replaced since they first came into existence—they have been known throughout Japan's long history as the Regalia and have always been recognized as the symbols of the right of the imperial family to rule.

II

The People
of the
Treasures

神話時代

2

The Land and the People

"CIPANGU," said Marco Polo in the year 1299, "is an island toward the east in the high seas, fifteen hundred miles from the continent; and a very good island it is."

He was in prison in Genoa at the time, dictating the story of his travels in the Far East to a companion, and it is from his memory of the three Chinese words *jih-pên-kuo,* sun- root- kingdom or the Kingdom of the Sunrise, that we get the word Japan. The Japanese themselves, however, call it Nippon which is their pronunciation of the first two of these same three Chinese syllables.

Widely travelled though he was, Marco Polo never went to Japan; and everything he wrote about it was hearsay. As a result, he was wrong about its distance from the mainland, as he was about many things. It is only a little over a hundred miles from

Korea to the main Japanese island of Honshu, and the greatest distance between the mainland and any of the four major islands that make up Japan proper is less than six hundred miles. These four islands, and a host of smaller ones, lie off the mainland in a long curve like a bow whose southern tip is just a little south of the Korean peninsula and whose northern tip reaches almost to the peninsula of Kamchatka.

Notwithstanding the Izanagi myth, the islands rose from below the surface of the sea rather than dropping down from above. For they are of volcanic origin and were thrust up by some titanic upheaval millions of years before the beginning of history.

Japan has often been compared to another important island country—England—which lies off the opposite shore of the vast Eurasian land mass. But Japan is much farther from the mainland; the Strait of Korea is four times as wide as the English Channel between Dover and Calais. There are other important differences. Japan is much more mountainous than England, the result of its volcanic origin. In fact, there is almost no part of Japan that is not within sight of mountains. And it lies farther to the south than England. The four main islands stretch for about 1,300 miles in an arc between about the same latitudes in our country as Georgia on the south and the Canadian border on the north.

A final difference is size. Though we, and the Japanese themselves, tend to think of Japan as small, it is actually half again as large as the United Kingdom and about the size of the whole of Germany.

Japan is a green country, with many rivers as well as many mountains. It lies within the monsoon belt, which means that in the late spring and early summer warm winds blow in from the Pacific, bringing a great deal of rain, which is good for the growing rice. But in the winter the wind blows from Siberia and it gives the northwest coast of Honshu an extremely heavy snowfall for that particular latitude.

This, then, is the land: mountainous but fertile with an extremely long coast line washed by seas that teem with fish. What about the people?

Little is known about the earliest people of Japan. The Ainu, a hairy, bearded and white-skinned people who now live almost exclusively in the far north of Japan, are generally considered to be the descendants of one of the groups of early settlers. Their resemblance to certain types of Russians has often been noted.

It is known that some Stone Age people lived in the mountains, where they hunted and ate nuts, roots, and berries; and others, a larger group, appear to have lived on the seashore and on the banks of rivers and lakes and eaten fish, shellfish, and seaweed.

This early culture continued until a fairly late date—about 200 B.C.—and by then it had reached quite a high level. Some Japanese scholars claim that it was one of the most advanced Stone Age cultures in the world in the design of its pottery and bone weapons. Nevertheless it was still a primitive society, and by 200 B.C. many countries in many other parts of the world were much further along the road to civilization; Socrates had been dead for two hundred years by then; the Great Pyramid of Gizeh had been standing for over two thousand years; and more important to Japan, parts of the great wall of China had been standing for over a hundred years.

About 200 B.C. there was a migration to Japan

from the mainland by a nomadic people, primitive by Chinese standards, who had been kept out of China by the Great Wall. They moved south into Korea and then across into Japan. Although considered barbarians by the Chinese, they were much more advanced than the people then living in Japan, for they had learned how to work metal. They were known as the Tomb People because of the large mounds in which they buried their dead. Outside the mounds, probably to protect the dead from evil spirits, they placed strange clay figures called *haniwa,* so they were also known as the *Haniwa* people.

The faces and costumes of the haniwa figures are generally Northern Asiatic, and the bronze and iron armor and weapons found in the tombs show a debt to the Chinese and Mongolians. Among other objects found in the tombs were *magatama* or comma-shaped jewels, either ornaments or objects for ceremonial use, that were curved like the claws or tusks of animals. These magatama were beautifully carved of semi-precious stone; in many cases of stone that is not found in Japan or even China, but is common in parts of

Russia. Until recently the claw of the tiger, which the magatama resembles, was considered an amulet of great power in Korea and eastern Siberia.

All this is clear evidence of a migration to Japan from the north. But there is also evidence, though it is not quite so concrete, of migrations from the south. This can be found in the Japanese language, in their houses, agriculture, and attitude toward nature, in some of their physical characteristics, and in their myths and legends.

Scholars still find the Japanese language a mystery for it bears no clear-cut relationship to any other known language. There are northern and east-central Asiatic elements in it, but there are also elements in it that appear to be Polynesian. Uninformed people mistakenly believe that the Japanese and Chinese languages are alike because the characters used in writing are similar. But this came about because the Japanese had no writing of their own and adopted the Chinese ideographs, which are primarily symbols. Actually the Japanese language is quite different from the Chinese. Many Japanese words, especially nouns, resemble words used in Malaya and Polynesia.

The type of house in which people live usually changes very slowly in form and reflects the climate of the country. Japanese houses are all comparatively open. They are hardly the kind that people living in the generally cold areas of Korea and the Asiatic mainland would have developed. This, too, would indicate that at least some of the Japanese people must have come from a warmer, southern region. Even more important is the wet method of rice growing used by the early Japanese. It seems to have originated in South China, for it is not at all common in the north.

Some parts of the early Japanese myths—the curved Sacred Jewel, for instance, one of the Three Treasures, which is obviously a magatama—seem to have come with the northern people. Other parts of myths—the character of the gentle sun and nature goddess, Amaterasu, and her concern for the rice fields—seem to come from the southern culture, for rice is a southern food and it is unlikely that immigrants from Korea would have been familiar with it at an early date.

From all this evidence we can say that, after the earliest people, the islands were settled by a series of people, some of whom came up from the south and some from the north. The majority of the people of Japan are from the north. They are of Asiatic stock—probably Mongolian—and came to the islands by way of the Korean peninsula.

The story of Susanowo and the eight-tailed dragon seems to agree with this theory of migration and occupation. There is almost always some underlying truth in myths and legends, and scholars generally agree that hidden in this particular legend is the story of an actual historical chieftan. The dragon could be a river with eight branches, destructive of life and property when it was in flood, and the magic sword a deposit of iron found at the end of one of its tributaries. The invading people, metal workers, made weapons of the iron, which seemed miraculous to the less civilized inhabitants of the district.

Later, at about the end of the first century, A.D., certain *uji* or clans of Kyushu, Japan's southernmost island, either conquered their neighbors or combined with them and pushed their way east until they reached the province of Yamato on the main Japanese island of Honshu. There they established Japan's first central state and either conquered or combined again with another group of people in the Izumo district who were also of South Korean stock. It is from these groups that the rulers of Japan have come for almost two thousand years.

3

The Beginnings

ONE OF the first references to Japan and the Japanese people that we have comes from a Chinese source, the records of the great Han dynasty. Its date is about 57 A.D. and it first describes the arrival of a Japanese ambassador at Loyang, capital of the Han colony in Korea. It then goes on to say:

"The country of the Wa lies southeast of South Korea in the middle of the ocean and is formed of a number of islands. It contains more than a hundred kingdoms. From the time when the Emperor Wu-ti conquered Chao-hsien (North Korea, in 108 B.C.), more than thirty of these kingdoms have held intercourse with China by envoys or by scribes. The people of the Wa understand the art of weaving. Their soldiers have spears and shields, wooden bows, and bamboo arrows sometimes tipped with bone. The men all tattoo their faces and adorn their bodies with designs. Differences of rank are indicated by the position and size of the pattern. They smear their bodies with pink and scarlet, as rice powder is used in China."

Later records—of the third century—speak of a Japanese queen named Pimiku. The men of this period still tattoo their faces and work designs on their bodies. However now, "They have arrowheads of iron as well as of bone. They use only an inner and no outer coffin. They have distinctions of rank and some are vassals of others. Taxes are collected. There are markets in each province where they exchange produce for other articles which they want."

Some years later, when Queen Pimiku died, "A great mound was raised over her, more than a hundred paces in diameter, and over a thousand of her male and female attendants followed her in death. Then a king was raised to the throne, but the people would not obey him and civil war broke out, not less than a thousand people being slain."

This would indicate that while a state had been established in Yamato, it was not yet strong enough to rule over the greater part of Japan.

Shortly after this the great Han empire, which had been in existence for four hundred years, broke up into three rival kingdoms. With the Chinese strength divided, the various small kingdoms of Korea began a struggle to seize the rich treasures of Loyang. As the warfare continued, conditions on the mainland became so unsettled that whole villages, including scholars, artists and workmen of all kinds, began moving to Japan in search of a more peaceful life.

These newcomers had many skills that the Japanese did not have. They knew how to make glass and lacquer, weave and dye silk, and how to fertilize the soil in order to raise more and better crops. But, most important, many of them knew how to read and write. The Japanese rulers soon adopted the Chinese written language officially. This meant that they could now begin to keep records, write laws and orders, and so begin to develop an effective central government.

Because of their knowledge and skills, the new emigrants from the mainland were greatly honored, given land on which to build homes, and were also often given official rank and important posts in the government. With such favored treatment they prospered, increased in numbers, and began to play an important role in Japan's growth as a nation. By the year 540, records show, there were seven thousand T'sin households in Japan—about a hundred thousand people; and by the end of the seventh century, one fourth of the noble families listed in the Japanese peerage were either of Chinese or Korean descent.

One of the many things that the newcomers from the mainland brought with them was Buddhism. The native Japanese religion, a form of nature worship, had never been organized into any sort of system. In fact, until this time, it did not even have a name. But many Japanese resisted the new ideas. The resistance was led by two important Yamato families, the Nakatomi, which had been responsible for the proper performance of all religious ceremonies for many generations, and the Mononobe, one of the leading military families. They now gave their cult a name, calling it *Shinto* or the Way of the Gods, and did everything they could to perpetuate it and discourage the growth of Buddhism. When a plague broke out about the middle of the sixth century, they claimed it was because the kami or native gods were angry, and a famous statue of Buddha was thrown into a canal and his shrine burned.

Buddhism had the support of another important family, however, the Soga. The Soga were also an ancient and noble clan. They were particularly important during this period because they were in charge of the imperial estates. They had employed many of the new arrivals from the continent and were extremely sympathetic to their religion, becoming the first native Japanese family to accept Buddhism.

Interest in Buddhism continued to grow, and it became firmly established about the year 600 when Prince Shotoku, who had been studying Buddhism and the Chinese classics for many years, became regent for his aunt, the Empress Suiko.

Shotoku was a remarkable man. In an attempt to end the struggle for power among the large landowners and the important clans, he drew up a code which is sometimes called the Seventeen Article Constitution. With this he hoped to give Japan a stable government similar to China's. The points in the code were more moral than political, indicating the value of harmony and listing some of the responsibilities of the ruler and the ruled. Although many of the precepts of the code were ignored, it had an important effect because it was the first attempt to set down a theory of government in Japan. It stated for the first time that "The Sovereign is master of the people of the whole country, and the officials to whom he gives authority are his vassals."

Under Shotoku there was a tremendous growth of interest in all forms of Chinese culture—literature, painting and music—and it was at this time that the

Chinese calendar was adopted. It has been said that all cultures borrow from one another, but usually only a little at a time, as one borrows a cup of sugar from a neighbor. Japan, however, was a wholesale borrower from an early date and continued to borrow for centuries after this.

When Shotoku died in 621, the Soga clan, which had grown to great importance under him, seized power and began deciding who should sit on the throne, not hesitating to murder those who stood in their way.

But the rule of the Soga did not last. Nakatomi no Kamatari, a man as remarkable in his way as Shotoku had been, was to bring about their downfall. It is the custom of the Japanese to put their family name first, before their given name, therefore Kamatari was a member of the Nakatomi family. The leaders of the family were the hereditary priests of the Shinto religion, which had lost much of its influence and prestige when Buddhism became so powerful under Shotoku and the Soga. Since Buddhism had come from China, Kamatari might have resented and resisted everything that was Chinese. But he was too intelligent a man for that. The T'ang Dynasty had just come into power in China and had made it the largest, most powerful, and best governed country in the world. Kamatari studied the Chinese system of government and determined to break the power of the Soga and give Japan a government similar to China's. But he needed help, powerful help.

Because of his family's hereditary religious role, he knew all the imperial princes. Prince Naka seemed to be the most promising of them, the one most likely to agree with his views.

His first opportunity to talk to the prince came during a football game. What the Japanese called football at that time was nothing like any game that we play, but was an exercise of individual skill in which the player kicked the ball into the air and tried to keep it from touching the ground for as long as possible.

One day, while Prince Naka was performing at this for members of the court, one of his shoes flew off. Picking it up, Kamatari kneeled and offered it to the prince. Though the prince could not know that in doing so Kamatari was symbolically offering him the whole of the kingdom, he graciously took the shoe from Kamatari. From that time on the two young men were fast friends and were constantly seen together deep in talk, supposedly about the Chinese classics in which they were both interested.

Actually, what they were doing was plotting the overthrow of the Soga. The first step in the plan as outlined by Kamatari was for Prince Naka to marry the daughter of Kurayamada, an important Soga, and thus enlist his aid.

When Prince Naka had done this, they were ready for the next step. Here, while their objectives may have been good, their methods were no better than those of the family they opposed. For their plan was to have Iruka, the head of the Soga clan, killed at a court reception.

On the day selected, Kurayamada, Prince Naka's father-in-law, appeared before the empress and, with Iruka standing by, began to read three memorials from the Kingdom of Korea. Once the attention of the court was engaged, Prince Naka ordered the guards to close the gates and allow no one else to enter the palace grounds. Then, calling them together, he offered them large rewards not to interfere in what was going to happen. When they agreed, he entered the hall and gave a signal to the two lords who were to do the actual killing. But the lords, awed by the presence of the empress and the enormity of the crime they had agreed to commit, made no move.

Kurayamada continued reading, but, afraid that no action would be taken and the plot would fail, he began to perspire profusely. Iruka, always a suspicious man, asked him what was wrong. Kurayamada explained that he was perspiring because of the strain involved in being in the august presence of the empress.

Again Prince Naka signaled to the two conspirators. When they still made no move, he drew his own sword and cut at Iruka, wounding him. This gave one of the lords the courage he needed, and he drew and attacked Iruka also.

"What is the meaning of this outrage?" cried the empress in horror as Iruka fell at her feet.

"It was for you and the imperial family that we did it," said Prince Naka. "For Soga Iruka wished to destroy the Celestial House and rule instead of the imperial descendants."

The empress looked at Prince Naka, at Iruka lying dead at her feet, and—possibly in fear, but certainly aware of her helplessness—withdrew to her private quarters.

The plot had succeeded. The Soga had been greedy and open in their usurpation of power and many clans had given them unwilling obedience. These clans now came over to the side of Prince Naka and Kamatari. Within the next few days most of the other Soga leaders had been killed also and their fortresses burned.

Prince Naka and Kamatari did not take power

in their own names. They knew if they did so it would only be a matter of time before they would be challenged by one of the other clans, as they themselves had challenged the Soga. There was only one family whose right to rule could not be questioned, the imperial family. Therefore, the two forced the empress to abdicate and placed her younger brother, Prince Naka's uncle, on the throne. He became the Emperor Kotoku and named Prince Naka as his heir. But while he may have been called the emperor, the true rulers of Japan were the two steadfast and farseeing men who had put him on the throne.

Guided by Prince Naka and Kamatari, the emperor issued an edict which gave this period the name of *Taikwa* or the Great Reform. Under the provisions of this edict, administration by local chieftans was to be abolished and all property returned to the emperor; a central government was to be organized with a capital on the Chinese pattern; all parts of the country were to be linked by a system of roads and ferries; a census was to be taken and records kept of the land given to the people for their use; the old taxes and forced labor formerly owed to the clan chiefs were now to be paid to the central government.

Prince Naka set an example by turning over his lands to the emperor, and many of the large landowners followed his lead. In return, they were made governors or administrators of their former territories or estates and paid for their services by the emperor. This tied them closely to the central government and made it stronger than it had ever been before.

In the year 668, Prince Naka mounted the throne as the Emperor Tenchi. He became emperor reluctantly, for he felt he could be more effective if he were not actually on the throne, but the power behind it. Meanwhile Kamatari had been rewarded with large estates. His family came to be called Fujiwara, which is the Japanese word for the wisteria under which Prince Naka and Kamatari used to meet, and that name became one of the greatest and best known in Japan.

Though the way in which Prince Naka came to power was violent and bloody, he was sincere in his desire to do what he could for his country and, as a result, he was much loved as emperor. That he in turn loved and understood his people is shown by one of the poems he wrote about the difficult life of the poor farmers:

> *Crudely thatched*
> *Is the roof of the hut*
> *At the autumn rice fields.*
> *My clothes are wet*
> *With the rain that drips through.*

The changes Naka brought about influenced every part of Japanese life. Not the least affected were military traditions. Always before, every able-bodied male in the nation had been a soldier to be called on for service in time of need, and the emperor himself was the commander-in-chief. Now, however, for the first time a distinction was made between the civil government and the military command; between the *kuge* or court nobles and the *buke* or knights. Generals were appointed, a War Office organized, and military districts established. The only qualifications needed to bear arms were physical, with the youngest and strongest being the most in demand. And since military service was only for a limited period during which no taxes were paid, there were always men available for military duty. There was no hereditary class of warriors yet nor did any one group have the exclusive right to bear arms.

Another result of the Great Reform Edict was the building of a capital. Before this, the seat of government had been located in different places, depending on where the emperor or empress happened to live. Now, in the year 710, the court moved to Nara which was in the northern part of Yamato, about halfway between Ise and the present port of Osaka. Here Japan acquired not only a capital, but a city such as it had never known before. Set in a pleasant valley, it was laid out in a rectangle with wide, straight avenues on the plan of the Chinese capital, Ch'ang-an. While it was being built, skilled workmen poured into the area, not only from Japan, but from the continent as well. Later, artists and sculptors came to help make the palaces of the imperial family and the court officials even

more beautiful. And, when their work was finished, many of the artists and craftsmen stayed on, so that Nara became the artistic and cultural, as well as the political capital of Japan.

The Nara period, which lasted for about seventy-five years, saw the first great flowering of Japanese civilization. During this time the court reached a high level of sophistication. Beautiful costumes, patterned on the latest Chinese fashions were worn and elaborate ceremonials indulged in. The *Kojiki* or Record of Ancient Matters and the *Nihongi* or Chronicles of Japan were completed during this time, works which together traced the history of Japan from its mythical beginnings to that day.

While the Nara period was a time of great and rapid growth for all of Japan, those who benefited most from it, especially after the death of Naka and Kamatari, were the Buddhists. There was good reason for this. Following their acceptance at the imperial court under Prince Shotoku, they had steadily become more important and influential. Buddhist temples and monasteries became large, richly endowed institutions. The Buddhist priests were generally the most learned men of their time. Since they knew how to read and write, they were skilled in medicine, engineering, metallurgy, and the arts as well as religion. They not only worshipped and taught at their temples and monasteries, they also treated the sick and took care of orphans and the aged. This made them popular with the common people.

When a smallpox epidemic broke out, the Buddhists took advantage of it by saying that the only hope for the salvation of Japan lay in Buddha. The emperor immediately ordered additional temples to be built in every province, and work was begun on a bronze statute of Buddha that was more than fifty feet high. It was completed and placed in a specially built sanctuary in the year 752.

Seventeen years later, the Buddhists reached the peak of their power during the reign of the Empress Koken when a monk named Dokyo moved into the imperial palace and was given the highest rank in the realm. But this was not enough for him. He announced that the Shinto god, Hachiman, had appeared to him in a vision and declared that if he, Dokyo, were made emperor, Japan would enjoy eternal prosperity and peace. The empress, however, decided to consult Hachiman herself and sent an emissary to his shrine. The reply came back that, since Dokyo was not of imperial lineage, he could not become emperor. Dokyo was furious and had the emissary banished, but his influence was weakened considerably, and when the empress died shortly after that, Dokyo was banished himself.

Following the death of the empress, the Fujiwara came back as chief advisors. They were very influential under the next emperor, the elderly Konin, and when he died they selected his successor, another of the re-markable men in Japanese history, the Emperor Kwammu.

Kwammu was a great grandson of the Emperor Tenchi and a very learned man. He had been the head of the imperial university at Nara, which was chiefly concerned with the study of the Chinese theories of government and the responsibilities of rulers to their people. This was one of the chief reasons the Fujiwara favored him.

When Kwammu became emperor, he began making plans to move the capital from Nara. The chief reason was probably the desire of Kwammu and the Fujiwara to get away from the Buddhists, whose power was centered in Nara. For though they were Buddhists themselves, they were not happy about Buddhism's great influence.

The Buddhists and many of the clan leaders fought the move, but in 784 the capital was established in Nagaoka. Ten years after that it was moved to still another site, one that was to remain the capital for four hundred years. This new site, some thirty miles north of Nara, was called Heian-kyo, the Capital of Peace. It still exists as Kyoto. The two hundred years that followed its establishment are known as the Heian period. It was a time when Japanese arts and culture surpassed even the Nara period.

When Kwammu took the throne, he faced many problems. One of them was finances. The Nara government had not been too concerned about the collection of taxes and had permitted large areas of land to come into the hands of priests and nobles who did not pay taxes, thus reducing the state's income. Kwammu reorganized the country's tax collecting methods and issued an edict forbidding the gift or sale of land to religious organizations.

Another of his problems was the Ainu, the original inhabitants of Japan, who had all been driven up into the northern portion of Honshu, Japan's main island. During the reign of Kwammu's father, the Ainu had been joined by rebellious farmers. Together they had not only refused to pay taxes, but had also begun raiding southward. They were fierce fighters who "gathered together like ants, but dispersed like birds." Furthermore, they had already won two victories over the imperial troops.

In 794, the year the court moved to Kyoto, Kwammu took a drastic and unusual step. Until this time, when any military measures were required the emperor himself or one of the imperial princes had always led the armies. But in this case the need for a trained leader was so great that Kwammu appointed a chief of one of the military houses as *Seii-Tai-Shogun* or Barbarian-Subduing-General. Kwammu gave him a sword that symbolized full power to act against the Ainu. The move was successful. The Shogun lived up to his name, subduing the barbarians and driving them north until their leaders fled to the northernmost island of Hokkaido.

This was the first time that the title *Shogun* and the powers that went with it had ever been given to anyone. When this first Shogun had accomplished his task, he returned to the emperor the sword that had been given him as a symbol of his authority, and his commission was ended.

However, this time of national peril caused other changes in the military system that did not end. Since the role of the soldier had become more important than ever before, selective conscription was introduced. The strongest were called on to bear arms, and the weaker were permitted to continue to work.

After this, life and culture, also took a new turn in Japan. Between the years 600 and 800 the Japanese had borrowed much from the Chinese. They had taken over the Chinese script and adapted it to their own language. They had adopted Buddhism, and they had tried to establish a centralized government on the Chinese pattern. Towards the end of the ninth century, however, the enlightened T'ang Empire in China began declining and, feeling that there was little more to be learned from the mainland, the Japanese imperial court stopped sending envoys and students there. Instead, they began developing what they had learned along their own lines. A culture that was truly Japanese and not imitative began to emerge.

This period reached its high point shortly after the year 1000. Japanese sculptors carved statues that were not only more Japanese, but more beautiful than any that had ever been seen before; and new schools of painting arose. But our best picture of what court life was like in those days comes to us from the literature of the period.

By this time the Japanese had modified and simplified the written forms that they had borrowed from the Chinese so that they represented Japanese words, and with this script the women of the imperial court began writing works that were as natural and graceful as the way they talked. These works are still considered the classical literature of Japan. Here, for instance, is a short scene from *The Tale of Genji,* by Lady Murasaki, the story of the loves of Prince Genji, the son of the emperor, in a translation by Arthur Waley.

"Rokujo pulled aside the bed-curtains and tossing her hair back over her shoulders looked out into the garden. So many lovely flowers were growing in the borders that Genji halted for a while to enjoy them. How beautiful he looked standing there, she thought. As he was nearing the portico the maid who had opened the shutters came and walked by his side. She wore a light green skirt exquisitely matched to the season and place; it was so hung as to show to great advantage the grace and suppleness of her stride. Genji looked round at her.

"Let us sit down for a moment on the railing here in the corner," he said.

She seems very shy, he thought, but how charmingly her hair falls about her shoulders."

Reading this work now, it is difficult to believe that it was written when it was: more than fifty years before the Norman Conquest of England.

The Heian period is also known as the period of the Fujiwara. For during this time they were always the power behind the throne, selecting the emperors who were usually no more than figureheads to be replaced at will, and keeping the actual power in their own hands. This meant, of course, that they had to live in the capital, far from their hereditary lands. They turned over the job of maintaining order and collecting taxes in the provinces to other clans, principally the Taira and the Minamoto. These naturally surrounded themselves with men who had made a career of soldiering. Soon professional soldiers, copying the customs of their superiors, began handing on their functions to their sons, and so a number of military families began developing in the shadows of the great country families.

As the strength of the provincial nobility grew, the separation between the soldier and the peasant became sharper; and about the middle of the tenth century the term *samurai,* which means *"one who serves"* and was originally applied to the royal guard, acquired a special significance. It became the term used to describe the military magnates and their followers.

The strength of the great provincial families grew at this time not only because of their increasing military power, however, but also because they were not at court. They did not have to tax their farmers heavily in order to live the rich and extravagant life of the capital. As a result, they were not only well-liked by their own peasants, but their holdings constantly increased as other farmers ceded land to them, preferring to work for them rather than for court families. The Taira and the Minamoto were most fortunate in this respect. They became widely known. Since the Chinese symbol that stood for the Taira was pronounced *Hei* in Japanese and the Minamoto symbol was pronounced *Gen,* they were also known as the Heike and the Genji, both *ke* and *ji* meaning family or clan.

About the middle of the twelfth century, the Taira and the Minamoto became conscious of their own strength and of the weakness of the central government. From that time on they engaged in a great struggle for power with one another. It is this struggle that ended the Heian period and began one of the most colorful and exciting times in Japanese history; the period which gives us the story of handsome and dashing Yoshitsune and his comrade-in-arms, the giant monk Benkei.

4

The Heroes and the Treasures

IN A few hours it would be dawn and Benkei, at his post near the Gojo bridge on the outskirts of the capital, was becoming more and more discouraged. Not one samurai had come that way all night. Not that that was surprising. It was several weeks now since he had strode into the shop of the swordsmith, Munenobu, and told him what sort of weapon he wanted. And Munenobu, studying the huge monk who looked stronger than six men, had said, "For such a sword as you require, I would have to melt down one thousand ordinary swords. Get them for me, and I will make you what you want."

"One thousands swords?" said Benkei.

"Yes," said Munenobu. "For it is only points and edges that take the proper temper, and those are the only parts I would use in your weapon."

"Very well," said Benkei. "Then I will bring you one thousand swords."

And so had begun the strange reign of terror. Not that anyone was hurt, unless he resisted or showed fight when confronted by the gigantic apparition that loomed up out of the darkness and, in the politest terms, demanded his sword. In the beginning some had, of course, resisted. They had even gone out, singly or in groups, to hunt down the mysterious sword thief. But those who met him had been so badly knocked about that they were glad to escape without their swords, but with their lives. And when the greatest fencing master in the city went out to look for him and came back stripped of both sword and armor, the other samurai stopped going out at night altogether. Since the terrible sword thief was obviously more than human, and since he wore a monk's robes, he became known as the *Tengu Bozu* or goblin priest.

While Benkei was aware of the stir he had caused, this did not make him feel any better, for he was very close to the end of his task now. He had collected and turned over to the swordsmith nine hundred and ninety-nine swords. He needed only one more to complete the count, but it was beginning to look as if he would never get that last sword.

Suddenly he stiffened as he heard the soft, sad notes of a flute. He stepped back into the shadows, and a moment later the flute player appeared, a slim and graceful young man in white court dress. And, thrust through his sash, was a magnificent sword.

Benkei sighed with relief. He waited till the young man was on the bridge, then confronted him.

"I must say you're a bold fellow to be out at this hour," he said. "Have you never heard of the goblin priest? He stands before you now. But give me your sword and no harm will come to you."

The young man looked him up and down, interested, but not at all disturbed.

"Yes, of course I've heard of you," he said, "and I've wanted to meet you for some time. But I'm afraid I can't give you my sword. You see, it's a family heirloom. However, if you want it badly enough, you're welcome to try and take it."

Amused, and at the same time admiring the young man's courage, Benkei reached for the sword and was struck a sharp blow on the wrist by the flute. Furious, he raised his *naginata,* a halberd-like weapon with a long, curved blade.

"Very well," he growled. "If I must discipline you . . ." and he struck a terrible blow. But the young man was not there. He was standing ten feet away, fanning himself. Again Benkei cut, and again; but it was like trying to strike a butterfly with a barge pole, for the young man dodged every blow. Then, when Benkei's naginata bit so deeply into the rail of the bridge that he could not pull it free, the young man leaped in and struck him a staggering blow on the forehead with his iron-ribbed war fan. Dazed, Benkei tried to flee, but the young man tripped him up, then pounced on him, holding him down.

"Alas that I should ever live to see this day!" moaned Benkei. "That such a magnificent warrior should have appeared to lead the hated and decadent Taira clan! I am better off dead. Strike off my head. But first tell me your name."

Instead of drawing his sword, the young man helped Benkei to his feet.

'I am no Taira," he said. "I am Yoshitsune, eighth son of Minamoto Yoshitomo, and I have long been looking for someone like you to be my retainer. For, after myself, you are the greatest man-at-arms I have ever met."

Thus, the old tales tell us, did Yoshitsune and Benkei meet. And while some parts of their story may sound like folklore or a medieval romance, there is no question but that they were historical figures; that they did live and meet and, having met, remained constant companions, devoted to each other for the rest of their lives.

The struggle for power between the Taira and the Minamoto had become acute during the middle of the twelfth century when Kiyomori, the head of the Taira clan, had been made Shogun. His principal rival was the Minamoto chieftan, Yoshitomo, commander of the imperial guard. During a battle with the Taira, Yoshitomo was killed. So were two of his sons. But several other sons were not. One of these was called Yoritomo. His life was spared because Kiyomori's stepmother thought he resembled one of her children. The other was Yoshitsune, son of one of Yoshitomo's concubines. She was a beautiful woman; and when she pleaded for her child's life, Kiyomori spared him.

When his father was killed, Yoritomo had become head of the Minamoto clan. Knowing that he might prove dangerous one day, Kiyomori put him in the custody of the Taira chief, Hojo Tokimasa, who lived in the Mount Fuji area. However, Tokimasa did not like the way things developed in the capital and when Yoritomo eloped with his daughter, Tokimasa and his followers joined with what remained of the Minamoto forces to oppose the Taira. Yoritomo set himself up in the fishing village of Kamakura, about thirty miles south of the present day Tokyo, and began building up his strength. A practical man, Yoritomo had practical reasons for basing himself here. At Kamakura he was surrounded by friendly clans and could remain at a safe distance from Kyoto, which was the center of power of the Taira.

Yoshitsune had been put into a Buddhist monastery, but even as a boy he knew that he did not want to become a monk. As soon as he was old enough, he had escaped from the monastery and gone to the wild and distant north where he had found shelter with a friendly Fujiwara nobleman named Hidehira. Though still in his teens, he was already a magnificent swordsman, and he had begun to study military strategy.

When he had learned all he could from the most experienced chieftans in the north, he had gone back to
Kyoto, the capital, in disguise to continue his studies in
the Taira stronghold.

It was shortly after this that the famous meeting
with Benkei took place on the Gojo bridge. Benkei, a
strong partisan of the Minamoto, had not only been
in a monastery, also, but had become a monk before
he decided that the purely religious life was not for him.

After their meeting, Yoshitsune and Benkei gathered together a band of warriors who were eager as
they were to fight the Taira. The entire group went
north to the protection of Hidehira. Shortly after they
arrived in the north, Kiyomori, the cunning and ruthless head of the Taira, died, and the leadership of the
clan was taken over by the much less clever Munemori.
He sent an expedition against Yoritomo, but it was
defeated by the third of the important Minamoto leaders, Yoritomo's cousin, Yoshinaka.

Hearing of all this activity, Yoshitsune asked
Hidehira for troops so he could go south and join his
half-brother, whom he had never met. Hidehira tried
to restrain him, telling him that the time was not yet
ripe for a move against the Taira. But Yoshitsune was
insistent; and finally, after warning him to watch both
Yoritomo and Yoshinaka, Hidehira gave him fifteen
hundred men.

The meeting between the half-brothers took place
at Yoritomo's camp about two weeks later. Yoritomo,
surrounded by his armored officers, sat on a dais covered with bear skins. Yoshitsune, wearing armor sewn
with indigo thread, approached him. On his head was
a helmet with a gold frontlet engraved with a circular
bamboo leaf pattern, the insignia of the Minamoto. He

carried one of the family's hereditary swords, the one Benkei had coveted, in a deerskin sheath. He bowed respectfully to his older brother, and Yoritomo was so impressed by him that he almost got up and bowed in return.

The brothers talked. Yoritomo was thirty-five at the time, Yoshitsune little more than half that. Yoritomo told Yoshitsune that their cousin Yoshinaka was on his way to the capital with a portion of the army. Yoritomo indicated he was not sure what Yoshinaka would do when he got there. Yoritomo suspected that once his cousin had driven out the Taira, he might try to seize power himself by having himself appointed Shogun. Yoritomo was evidently testing Yoshitsune and, forgetting Hidehira's warning, Yoshitsune said, "If he should do that and—as head of the Minamoto—you should not want to lead an attack against him yourself, I will be glad to do it for you."

Reassured, Yoritomo took Yoshitsune back to Kamakura with him, and what he had expected soon took place. As Yoshinaka approached the capital, the Taira, led by Munemori, fled to the southwest, taking the child-emperor, Antoku, with them and also the Regalia, the Three Treasures of Japan: the Sacred Mirror, the Sword, and the Jewel. The Taira went first to the westernmost island of Kyushu but, finding the clans there unfriendly, moved to the island of Shikoku.

Yoshinaka at once tried to put an emperor of his own choosing on the throne. But the old ex-emperor, Go Shirawaka, was too clever for him and installed one of his own grandsons, Go Toba. Yoshinaka was furious, but such was the reverence in which an ex-emperor was held that there was nothing he could do about it. However, in revenge, he turned his fierce mountain troops loose in the capital to loot and pillage as they wished. The only person who could possibly control Yoshinaka was Yoritomo, and Go Shirawaka appealed to him for help.

This was what Yoritomo had been waiting for, and he sent his troops to take the capital from Yoshinaka. However, never willing to trust anyone completely, he divided the command between Yoshitsune and another of his brothers, Noriyori. After some hard fighting in which Yoshitsune showed his generalship as well as his swordmanship and courage, his forces approached the capital and Yoshinaka fled.

It was dark and, since it was winter, the rice fields were covered with a sheet of ice. Wandering off the road, Yoshinaka's horse broke through the ice into the deep mud and, while it floundered there, an arrow pierced Yoshinaka's helmet, killing him. Running up, the Minamoto soldiers cut off his head. Seeing this, Yoshinaka's last retainer, who had been fighting bravely to cover his master's retreat, cried, "Now who is there left for me to follow? Watch, you men of the east, and see how a warrior dies!" Putting the point of his sword in his mouth, he threw himself off his horse.

The Minamoto warriors then cut off his head, too, put them both in special head boxes, and sent them to Yoritomo.

Yoshitsune rode into the capital where he was greeted with great enthusiasm by Go Shirawaka in the name of the new, four-year-old puppet emperor. He praised Yoshitsune for what he had done and asked him to protect the capital from the Taira who had gained strength and moved back to the mainland, establishing themselves in the strong fort at Ichinotani, near Kobe. Go Shirawaka not only wanted the Taira destroyed but, almost as important, he wanted Yoshitsune to win back the Three Treasures from them, for without them the child-emperor could not be properly crowned.

Yoshitsune sent to Kamakura for permission to do this. But, when Yoritomo delayed in answering, Yoshitsune moved to the attack anyway. This campaign was one of his greatest, for the Taira were not only in a strongly fortified position with the sea in front of them and supposedly impassible mountains behind them, but they actually outnumbered the Minamoto forces. Recognizing Yoshitsune's great military ability, Noriyori accepted his leadership; and Yoshitsune sent him with fifty thousand men to make a frontal assault on the Taira. He sent another twenty thousand men around the mountains to attack from the west, while he, Benkei and one hundred and eighty picked men crossed the mountains to see if they could find some way of attacking from the rear. With the aid of a local guide, they arrived at a steep and rocky bluff behind the Taira fort.

"Can a deer go down this?" Yoshitsune asked the guide.

"I have seen them go down it," the guide answered.

"Where a deer can go, our horses can go," said Yoshitsune, and he spurred his mount forward. Fighting had already begun and, with the unexpected appearance of Yoshitsune and his forces inside the fortifications, the Taira broke and fled in ships back to the island of Shikoku. But they lost enormous numbers of men and many of their leaders.

Becoming more and more convinced that Yoshitsune might be a dangerous rival, Yoritomo, still at

Kamakura, turned the command of his forces over to Noriyori. Yoshitsune was forced to return to the capital and remain there while Noriyori tried vainly to smash the Taira. When he not only failed to do this but was himself trapped, Yoritomo sent additional troops to the capital and let Yoshitsune take over. Yoshitsune landed on the island of Shikoku when the seas were so rough that the Taira did not expect him and won the battle of Yashima. But again, though many of the Taira were slain, most of them escaped in their ships, taking with them the Emperor Antoku and the Three Treasures which Yoshitsune had promised to regain for Go Shirawaka.

During this battle one of the many incidents took place that seemed to prophesy victory for the Minamoto. To taunt their enemies, one of the ladies of the Taira court fastened the child-emperor's fan to the mast of her ship. The ship was about a hundred yards or so from shore, but Yoshitsune called up one of his warriors who was a great archer. Riding into the sea, the archer raised his bow and aimed at the fluttering fan. His arrow flew true, smashing the fan, to the conster-

nation of the Taira.

The stage was now set for the battle of Dannoura, one of the most important in Japanese history. It took place on April 25, 1185. Gathering together a fleet of some seven hundred ships, Yoshitsune sailed west toward the narrow straits between the mainland and Kyushu, where the Taira forces were holding Noriyori. The Taira had about five hundred ships. Singing arrows flew between the vessels, signaling the beginning of the battle; and whenever the ships closed with one another the decks became red with blood. At first the battle did not go well for Yoshitsune's forces. The Taira were more experienced seamen. Then, suddenly, there was another omen. What at first looked like a white cloud, but then appeared to be a white banner, settled on the masthead of Yoshitsune's ship. At this, one of the Taira chieftains, with whom Yoshitsune had been intriguing, deserted to the Minamoto side with over two hundred ships and sent Yoshitsune a message telling him where he would find the emperor and the Three Treasures.

Now the tide of battle turned. Munemori and his son were taken prisoner, and Minamoto ships closed in on the junk that carried the young emperor and his grandmother. Thrusting the Sword through her girdle and putting the Jewel under her arm, the grandmother picked up Antoku and stepped to the gunwale.

"Though I am but a woman, I will not fall into the hands of the foe," she said. "Let those who have the courage follow me."

"Where are you taking me, Ama ze?" asked the anxious, eight-year-old emperor.

"There is a pure land of happiness beneath the waves," she said, "another capital where no sorrow is.

It is there that I am taking my lord." And saying the *Nembutsu*—the prayer for mercy and forgiveness—she leaped overboard with the child in her arms. Antoku's mother threw herself overboard, too, but was captured before she could sink.

The Minamoto warriors stormed aboard the junk. One of them found an ornately carved chest and opened it. Immediately his eyes darkened and blood gushed from his nose.

"Hold," said one of the captured Taira nobles. "For that is the Sacred Mirror that no profane eye may behold."

Awestruck, the warrior closed the chest.

So ended the battle of Dannoura—with the complete destruction of the Taira forces, the capture of Munemori, and the recovery of at least two of the Three Treasures. For the Jewel, in a wooden box like the Mirror, floated to the surface and was rescued from the sea. There is some question as to what happened to the Sword. Some chroniclers say that it was found by a diver the next day, some that it was not and that it was replaced by another sword the next year.

Yoshitsune returned to the capital in triumph and received honors that would have turned the head of a lesser man. He was now recognized as the greatest general in Japan and, what was more important, he was tremendously popular with the troops. These two facts were to cost him his life; for Yoritomo, still sitting in Kamakura, was aware of them and, now that the Taira had been destroyed, no longer had any need for Yoshitsune.

In June, Yoshitsune, Benkei and his retainers set out for Kamakura, taking Munemori and the other important Taira prisoners with them. When they reached a village about a mile from Kamakura, Yoshitsune received an order from Yoritomo to remain where he was, but to send on the prisoners. Yoshitsune was thunderstruck. Though a military genius, he was no psychologist. Completely loyal himself, he did not realize that his brother was jealous and afraid of him. He sent the prisoners on as directed, and they were barbarously slain. For three weeks Yoshitsune waited in the village. Most of his men, furious at the way he was being treated, wanted to advance on Kamakura and, if necessary, fight their way into Yoritomo's presence. But the cool-headed Benkei urged Yoshitsune to write his brother a letter. Yoshitsune did so, saying in part:

"These many days have I lain here and could not gaze upon thy face. The bond of our blood-brotherhood is sundered. But a short season after I was born, our honored sire passed to another world. Clasped in my mother's arms, I was carried to Yamato and since that day I have not known a moment free from care or danger. My life was wretched and perilous, for I had to hide myself where I could in all manner of places in distant provinces. But at last I was summoned to help in overthrowing the Taira, and in this conflict I first laid Yoshinaka low. Later I spurred my horse down frowning precipices and braved the dangers of wind and wave that threatened to make me the prey of the monsters of the deep. My helmet was my pillow, my weapons always at my hand and my sole desire was to please you and restore the fame of the Minamoto. I beg permission to make a direct appeal to you and hope that you will bestow on me words of kindness."

Instead of seeing him, Yoritomo ordered him back to the capital. Here he was offered new honors and appointments which Yoritomo directed him to refuse.

When he did not, Yoritomo sent a band of warriors to the capital to kill him. Yoshitsune fought off the assassins and uncovered the plot, but now he was convinced that he must take action to protect himself. When Yoritomo sent an army against him, he left the capital and went west to try and raise an army of his own. But now his luck changed. Trying to reach Shikoku, he was caught in a storm and most of his ships were wrecked. His own ship was driven back to the mainland in the neighborhood of Osaka. He was now truly at the mercy of Yoritomo.

After hiding in the hills for a time, Yoshitsune, his faithful and beautiful mistress, Shizuka, Benkei, and a few of his loyal retainers disguised themselves as wandering monks and began trying to work their way north to take shelter again with Hidehira. Discovering that Shizuka was about to have a child—his heir—and knowing that she could never stand the rigors of their cross-country march, Yoshitsune sent her back to the capital where he thought Go Shirawaka would protect her. She was captured, however, and sent on to Kamakura. When her child was born, a boy, as Yoshitsune had thought it would be, Yoritomo had it killed, but permitted Shizuka to retire to a nunnery. There, a year later, she died of a broken heart.

Meanwhile Yoshitsune, with Benkei and his few remaining men, had reached the outskirts of the capital. Yoshitsune, accompanied by Benkei, slipped into the city so he could say good-bye to his wife, the daughter of a Taira chieftan whom he had captured at Dannoura. To his dismay, he discovered that she was going to have a child also. If he left her, she would probably be killed and the child certainly would be, as that of Shizuka had been. Benkei took over. He himself cut off her long hair and dressed her as a boy so she could accompany them. At the same time, he suggested that Yoshitsune now assume a disguise as far from his true rank as possible, that of a coolie. Then they started north again.

By now Yoritomo's spies were everywhere, and every mountain pass and river crossing had guards watching for them. When they reached Ataka, they were stopped and questioned closely. Benkei was able to convince the warden at the barrier that they were indeed mendicant friars, accompanied by a few servants. But, as they started to go through the gate, the warden caught a glimpse of Yoshitsune's face under his broad-brimmed peasant's hat and became suspicious, finding it hard to believe that anyone who looked like that and carried himself so proudly could be a coolie. Sensing this, Benkei began shouting at Yoshitsune, calling him a lazy good-for-nothing and beating him with his staff. Reassured, the warden let them go through, for he was certain that a retainer would never dare lay hands on the sacred person of his lord.

Once they were safe, Benkei fell on his knees and begged Yoshitsune's pardon, offering to kill himself once he had guided them to the north. But, far from being angry with him, Yoshitsune embraced him, telling him he had saved all their lives and that he would always be both proud of him and grateful to him.

Feeling like men who have trod without harm on a tiger's tail or escaped a serpent's poisonous fangs, the little band continued north. High in a snowy pass, with Benkei as midwife, another son was born to Yoshitsune. When his wife was strong enough to be carried in a litter, they went on again. And at last they did reach Mutsu.

Hidehira took them in, as he had taken in Yoshitsune when he was a young man, giving him a castle and men to guard him. When Yoritomo learned that Yoshitsune had arrived safely in the north, he sent a messenger to Hidehira demanding that he give up Yoshitsune. But Hidehira refused, and he was so strong that Yoritomo dared not attack him. Then fate struck again, and Hidehira, now an old man in his nineties, died. His son, Yasuhira, was neither as loyal nor as courageous as Hidehira. Unwilling to take Yoshitsune as his liege lord and join him in a war against Yoritomo, which Yoshitsune might well have won, he decided to capture or kill Yoshitsune himself and then make terms with Yoritomo.

On June 15, 1189, when most of Yoshitsune's men were away, Yasuhira attacked. Though the defenders of the castle were few, two of them were Yoshitsune and Benkei and they were worth many hundreds. Yoshitsune raged through the battle like a demon. Where he was, there death was—not for him, though he seemed to court it—but for everyone he encountered. And Benkei, wielding his blood-stained halberd, was just as terrible. At nightfall they still held the fort, but they knew they could not last another day. Benkei offered to hold the ford at the river in front of the fort, vowing that no one would cross it that night, if Yoshitsune would escape to the north. Yoshitsune was reluctant, but finally agreed. However, when he, his wife, and son tried to do so, they discovered that they were surrounded. There was to be no escape for any of them.

Returning to the fort, Yoshitsune knelt before the small image of Buddha and prayed, then gave his dagger to one of his retainers. The retainer left the room and returned a few moments later with the dead body of his son. Yoshitsune's wife then knelt before him, saying, "I now have no child, no reason to continue living. Will you let me come with you where you are going?"

His eyes misty, Yoshitsune embraced her, said the *Nembutsu,* and killed her. Then seating himself in the correct position, he drove the dagger into the left side of his abdomen, drew it over to the right and gave the upward cut prescribed in *seppuku.** Thus, by his own hand, died Yoshitsune whose life, full as it was, had lasted less than thirty years.

Meanwhile Benkei, unaware of this, was holding the ford. Nearly a hundred men fell to his deadly halberd. With the morning's first light, Yasuhira's bowmen came up. They shot hundreds of arrows at him, but Benkei did not move; he stood there, still and menacing, with his back against a rock. It was his immobility that finally attracted more careful attention. Some of the bolder warriors rode into the stream and approached the motionless, giant figure. His body was riddled with war shafts until he resembled a porcupine. One of the arrows had struck him in the eye. So died Benkei. But even in death he had kept his word to his lord, for no man crossed the river during the night.

Yasuhira's treachery did him little good. Though he sent Yoshitsune's head to Yoritomo, Yoritomo still sent his troops north; and when they returned, they brought Yasuhira's head with them.

Yoritomo was now, without any doubt, the most important man in Japan. As such, the title of Shogun

---

* *Seppuku* is the classic word for ceremonial suicide. *Hara-kiri,* which means "belly-cutting," is a vulgarism and is not used in literature or polite speech.

was very important to him, for it would legitimatize the position he had seized by force of arms. But the Japanese reverence for the imperial family was so great that, even when he was the most powerful man in the country, he could not take the title. He had to wait until it was granted to him by the emperor. And that took until 1192—seven years after the battle of Dannoura. But then he not only got the emperor to give him the title, he also got him to make it hereditary.

Even when he had become Shogun, Yoritomo remained in Kamakura, not for sentimental reasons, but because he wanted to make sure that his warriors would not be influenced or corrupted by the soft life of the imperial court.

While he may have been cruel and self-seeking, Yoritomo was a good administrator. He set up a new type of feudal state whose structure was to last for one hundred and fifty years. Under the Shogun there were three separate departments. One was both a war and police department, responsible for maintaining order and punishing crime. A second was in charge of the general business of the government, including finances. And the third was both a court of justice and a form of legislature. By appointing military governors and land stewards, he was able to reward his supporters and extend his influence. At the same time he won the favor of both the Buddhist and Shinto priests by making gifts to both sects and rebuilding shrines that had been destroyed during the war with the Taira.

Once Kamakura became the administrative center of Japan, it began growing; and eventually, where there had been a small fishing village, there was a completely new city with a population of a quarter of a million.

For fifteen years Yoritomo was the absolute ruler

of Japan. And then it is possible that Yoshitsune had his revenge. For in 1198, when Yoritomo was at the height of his power and glory, his horse threw him when he was riding across a bridge. He was badly injured, lingered on in great pain till the following year, then died at the age of fifty-three. Those who were close to him insisted that the reason his horse had reared and thrown him was that both he and his horse had seen the ghost of Yoshitsune rising from the water under the bridge.

So died a crafty and ruthless man, who had had a profound effect on the history and institutions of his country. From this time on, until after the middle of the nineteenth century, though there was always an emperor on the throne, it was the Shoguns or military dictators who were the real rulers of Japan.

5

The Great Invasion
and the Divine Wind

IF YORITOMO had plotted, planned, and built in the
hopes of founding a dynasty, his hopes came to naught.
His two sons became Shogun in succession, inheriting
the title he had won for them; but both were murdered
and his widow and her father, Hojo Tokimasa, took
over the rule of the country.

Following this there came a period that was unique
even in Japanese history. It had become the custom to
have a dual system of government: an emperor sat on
the throne, but the actual power was in the hands of a
Shogun or military dictator. But now, for almost a
hundred and fifty years, there was a *triple* system of
government. For the Hojo—who could not inherit the
title of Shogun—became Regents, exercising the power
vested in the office of Shogun.

But Yoritomo had built well, for the country as a

whole if not for his descendants, and his decision to base himself at Kamakura had been a good one. While the nobles at the court at Kyoto continued to lead an idle and luxurious life, the military men worked hard, lived simply, and remained close to the people and their needs. Lawsuits were settled promptly and fairly, and efforts were made to reduce taxes. There was one attempt in 1221, by the ex-emperor Go Toba, to get the power away from the Hojo and bring it back to Kyoto; but this was taken care of when the Hojo sent an army to the capital.

In 1274, however, the Hojo Regents—and Japan as a whole—faced a test that few nations in the world had been able to endure. Early in the thirteenth century the Mongol hordes, under the blood-red flag of Jenghiz Khan, swept over most of Asia up to the banks of the Danube; and all of eastern Europe trembled before their might. By about 1234 they had conquered most of China. In the year 1260 Kublai Khan, the grandson of Jenghiz Khan, became Emperor of China and shortly after that he began looking to the east, toward the island empire of Japan.

It was not additional territory that Kublai Khan was interested in—he had more than enough of that—but trade. For several hundred years before there had been a considerable amount of trade between China and Japan. However, when Yoritomo had taken over in Kamakura, the imperial treasury was empty. The Hojo Regents who succeeded him were thrifty men who were satisfied with homemade things, so trade with China was stopped to preserve what was left of the national wealth. There were other ways of acquiring goods than by trade, however; and as trade ceased, Japanese pirates began sailing to the mainland and looting along the coasts of Korea and China. The Chinese and Korean governments had complained about this several times and on several occasions the Japanese government had ordered the pirates to return what they had stolen.

In 1268 Kublai Khan sent an envoy to Japan, carrying a letter from "the Emperor of Great Mongolia" to "the King of Japan," suggesting that Japan reopen friendly relations with China. He pointed out that when relations are not friendly, war follows. The message went, not to the emperor at Kyoto, but to Kamakura where the Regent was Hojo Tokimune, the sixth of his line. Angry at the tone of the message, Tokimune did not reply to it or to five additional messages that the great Khan sent him.

Despite the efficiency of the Kamakura administration, bad times had come on Japan. The country had been devastated and bankrupted by the wars between the Taira and the Minamoto and had never really recovered. Now conditions were aggravated by earthquakes, plagues, and famine. Comets blazed in the skies, seeming to warn of coming doom, and a Buddhist priest named Nichiren echoed that warning in the streets of Kamakura, telling all who would listen to repent and turn to the true faith of Buddha before disaster came.

Then, in October 1274, Kublai Khan struck. A fleet of about four hundred and fifty ships, carrying fifteen thousand Mongol troops and another fifteen thousand Korean seamen and auxiliaries, sailed from Korea. Their first contact with the Japanese was at Tsushima, an island halfway between Korea and Kyushu. The Japanese had been expecting an invasion, but the garrison at Tsushima was comparatively small and was not prepared for the type of warfare practised by the Mongols.

As the invaders stormed ashore, the Japanese met them on the beaches and even in the shallow water. But in addition to their superior numbers, the Mongols had weapons with which the Japanese could not cope; catapults, which were probably built for Kublai Khan by Marco Polo's father and uncle; and heavy cross-bows, mounted on the decks of their ships, that could shoot a huge dart several hundred yards. These weapons took a heavy toll of the defenders.

Once ashore the Mongols formed phalanxes, for they had been trained to fight in formation, presenting a solid front of metal shields to the warriors who awaited them. Though the Japanese were a warlike people, their method of fighting was totally different from the Mongols. They fought in very loose formation, or in no formation at all, and their battles consisted for the most part of a series of single combats. They did not realize that they were facing a body of men who cared nothing for honor or individual action, but were trained to kill as efficiently as possible.

A group of the best Japanese swordsmen, gay in their brightly colored armor of laminated iron and leather, advanced on the invaders to challenge them to single combat, as was their custom. Many of them were shot down by the fur-hatted Mongol crossbowmen. And when one of the Japanese did reach the enemy, instead of sending out a single man to answer the samurai's challenge, the Mongols opened their phalanx, surrounded him, and cut him to pieces.

Facing these tactics as well as new and strange weapons, the Japanese suffered appalling losses. Where they could engage the enemy in single combat or anything that approached it, the story was different. For the Japanese warrior was the equal of any fighting man anywhere in courage and skill, and the Japanese sword

was superior to any in the world.

Nevertheless, the weight of numbers told, and by sunset the few remaining defenders were exhausted. As the Mongols poured into the town, the governor, his family and the few remaining defenders took their own lives.

The Mongols burned the town, taking some prisoners but slaughtering most of the inhabitants; and two weeks later they attacked the island of Iki, which was about fifty miles away, halfway between Tsushima and Kyushu. Having gotten word of what had happened at Tsushima, the governor of Iki sent a fast boat to Kyushu asking for help and, at the same time, prepared to defend the island. The inhabitants were mostly fishermen or sailors and they joined with the garrison in its defense. But though they fought as bravely as the men of Tsushima and held out for a day and a night, the end was the same, and they were finally overwhelmed. The Mongol Armada then sailed for Kyushu.

When news of what happened on the two outer islands reached Kyushu, messengers on fast horses were sent to Kamakura. But, knowing that it would be a long time before fresh troops could possibly arrive, the people of Kyushu prepared to defend themselves. They had been ordered to fortify their coast some time before, when relations with the Mongols had begun deteriorating; and they now had ramparts along some thirty miles of shoreline. The local clan chiefs and estate stewards roused and armed every man they could and mustered them along the northern coast.

The troops at Kyushu had had four days warning and, barring reinforcements, were as prepared as they could be for the arrival of the Mongols. But they were

not prepared for the sight that met their eyes when the
Mongol ships appeared and cast anchor in Hakozaki
Bay. For the Mongols had taken hundreds of prisoners
that they had captured on Iki, both men and women,
stripped them naked, and nailed them by their hands
and feet to the bows of their ships. Outraged at this
sight, the Japanese left the shelter of their fortifications
and went storming down to the shore to meet the
invaders.

The initial advantage in an assault of this sort
lies with the attackers, for they can concentrate their
forces where they choose, while the defenders—not
knowing where the attack will come—must spread out
over a wide area. In addition, the Mongols now
brought into play still another weapon with which the
Japanese were unfamiliar—war drums. The thunderous
booming of these huge drums, brought along for this
very purpose, so terrified the Japanese horses that the
mounted knights could not control them, and as a
result the cavalry on the Japanese flanks was virtually
useless.

Despite these disadvantages, the outnumbered
Japanese troops continued to hold the Mongols to the
immediate vicinity of Hakozaki Bay for three days. On
the fourth day reinforcements arrived from Dazai-fu,
the capital of Kyushu; some three thousand men and
a flotilla of about three hundred small boats. Though
still outnumbered, the Japanese took heart from this
and fought so fiercely that when night came the Mongols retreated to the shelter of their ships.

Now the small Japanese fleet went into action.
Though the wind was rising, promising a storm, the
fleet sailed out to attack the great Mongol Armada.
The Japanese boats were all small, few of them carry-

ing more than a dozen men, while the Mongol ships carried hundreds. But the men on the small boats were skilled warriors as well as seamen, and besides, they now had a trick of their own up their sleeves. About fifty of their boats were fire ships, loaded to the gunwales with dry straw. Putting the torch to these, they sent the blazing crafts crashing into the closely packed mass of Mongol ships. Then, as the Mongols woke to find many of their ships ablaze, the Japanese poured a hail of arrows into them, picking off the invaders who were silhouetted against the leaping flames.

Harder and harder blew the wind until the Japanese, knowing what was coming, broke off the engagement and fled to the shelter of the shore. Then nature dealt the Mongols their final blow. For the rising wind was the forerunner of a great storm that smashed many of their ships on the rocks of the bay and sent the remainder flying for safety out to sea. By morning not a single enemy ship remained in Japanese waters. Those that were still afloat fled northward to Korea; and when Kublai Khan came to reckon up his accounts, he found that the expedition had cost him almost two hundred ships and over thirteen thousand men.

Now there was rejoicing throughout Japan, but the joy was tempered by anxiety. For no one—from the emperor and the Regent Tokimune down to the lowliest peasant—believed that the Great Khan would accept this defeat and let matters rest there. Orders went out to fortify additional sections of the Kyushu coast, and other orders called on the chieftans in that area to provide lists of men and arms they could supply when needed. Some of these lists have come down to us, and one of them gives a graphic picture of the household of an aged warrior:

*Saiko, aged eighty-five, cannot walk.
Nagahide, his son, aged sixty-five. Has bow
and arrows and weapons. Tsunehide, his son,
aged thirty-five. Has bow and arrows, weapons, corselet, one horse.*

*Matsujiro, kinsman, aged nineteen. Has
bow and arrows, arms and two followers.*

*Takahide, grandson, aged forty. Has
bow and arrows, weapons, corselet, one
horse, and one follower.*

*These are at His Lordship's orders and
will serve faithfully. Humbly presented as
above.*

April, 1276.

SAIKO.

However not everyone in Japan showed such
self-sacrificing patriotism. Many of the warriors now
began clamoring for a reward for the part they had
played in repelling the Mongols, and many of the
monasteries took advantage of the disturbed situation
to begin quarreling among themselves in disputes over
land. On the whole, though, the terrible threat from
outside did awaken a sense of national unity and most
of Japan, particularly the military class, responded
firmly and wholeheartedly. Then, in June, 1281,
Kublai Khan struck again.

This time the invaders sailed, not in one, but in
two huge fleets; one of about fifty thousand Mongols
and Koreans, from Korea, and one of about one hundred thousand Chinese, from southern China. The
Korean fleet tried to make landings close to the point
of the previous attack; and the southern fleet, arriving
a little later, attempted landings slightly to the south.

But the Japanese were not only better prepared this time, they had also learned a great deal from the earlier invasion attempt. Though they fought on the beaches when it was necessary, they did their best to keep the Mongols from landing. Time and again they sailed out in their small boats to attack the infinitely larger Chinese ships. Though many of the small craft were sunk by the Mongol catapults, others managed to reach the great ships and put all those on board to the sword.

One such exploit was carried out by a Japanese captain named Kono Michiari. Standing on the shore during the early days of the invasion, he saw a strange sight; a snow-white heron alighted on a turret of the Japanese fortifications, picked up an arrow in its beak, and, flying out, dropped it on one of the largest vessels in the enemy fleet.

"After such a sign from Hachiman," he said reverently, "who could fear death?"

Filling two small boats with his followers, he sailed out towards the anchored Mongol fleet. The Mongols, evidently believing that he was coming out to surrender, held their fire. Reaching the chosen Mongol ship, the Japanese cut down the masts of their small crafts and swarmed up them, using them as ladders to board the enemy vessel. Led by Kono Michiari, they fell on the invaders and—though they were outnumbered and suffered heavy losses—they killed all on board and set fire to the ship. Under cover of the smoke, those who remained rowed safely back to shore to the rage of the Mongols and the exultation of the Japanese.

For more than seven weeks the bloody fighting went on along the coast of Kyushu, and the fate of Japan hung in the balance. All during this time everyone in the kingdom who was not engaged in the fighting joined the emperor and the priests in praying for deliverance. The sound of the temple drums and the tinkle of the sacred bells was heard throughout the land, and the smoke of incense rose from every shrine, monastery, and temple. Early in August, the chief Shinto priest journeyed to the sacred shrine at Ise carrying a petition to the gods for aid from the emperor and the ex-emperor. He presented this at the shrine, offering up his own prayers as well.

Just before sunset that day a dark bank of clouds appeared in the sky, obscuring the sun. The wind began to rise and as night fell, weeks before such storms normally occur, a terrible typhoon blew in from the sea. It struck the closely packed ships of the Mongol fleet like an iron fist. Vessels were crushed together, dashed against the rocky shore, or overturned. For two days the wind blew, piling the wreckage of the once mighty fleet so tightly into the mouth of the bay it formed a bridge from shore to shore. For the second time Providence had intervened, coming to the aid of the courageous defenders of beleaguered Japan with what has been known ever since as the *Kamikaze* or Divine Wind.

Thus ended Kublai Khan's second attempt to invade Japan. One Japanese account says that of the four thousand ships only two hundred escaped, and that of the army of one-hundred-and-fifty thousand men only about one fifth returned safely to the continent. In addition to the Japanese and Chinese versions of the destruction of the Mongol fleet, we have that of Marco Polo, who wrote:

"And it came to pass that there arose a north wind which blew with great fury and caused great damage along the coast of the island, for its harbors were few. It blew so hard that the Great Khan's fleet could not stand against it. And when the chiefs saw that, they came to the conclusion that if the ships remained where they were, the whole navy would perish. So they all got on board and made sail to leave the country. But when they had gone about four miles they came to a small island on which they were driven ashore in spite of all they could do, and a large part of the fleet was wrecked and a great multitude of the force perished, so that there escaped only some thirty thousand men who took refuge on this island."

The parallel between the destruction of the Mongol fleet by the Divine Wind and the salvation of England from the Spanish Armada some three hundred years later is obvious. But, while the English had no continuing fear of the Spanish, the Japanese terror of the Mongols was so deeply imprinted that, until fairly recently, a Japanese mother would say to a crying infant, "Why are you afraid? Do you think the *moko* are coming?"

Again there was great rejoicing when the news of what had happened off Kyushu spread through Japan, but fear of yet another invasion attempt remained. This fear lasted for another twenty years. It was not until 1300, when Kublai Khan died, that the Japanese were convinced that the threat was gone forever.

Though the two invasion attempts failed, they had a profound effect on Japan. For almost three decades the resources of the country had been strained to keep her men-at-arms in the field, ready to repel the invaders. "During the past few years," says one contemporary account, "owing to the Mongol attacks, while warlike arts have not been neglected, agriculture has been practically abandoned by the peasants and landholders."

Once the danger was past, all those who had fought, and even those who had not, but claimed they were ready to, began clamoring for rewards. But the priests clamored loudest of all, claiming that it was their prayers that had raised the Divine Wind which had done more to save Japan than the swords of the warriors.

During the century or more that it had been in power, the Kamakura government had been able to survive because the wars it fought were civil wars, and it had been able to reward its supporters with the wealth and property it seized from its enemies. But there was no increase of wealth as a result of the wars with the Mongols, only expenditure and widespread destruction. In addition, the Hojo regents had now become decadent. Aware of the weakness in Kamakura, and realizing that their only hope of gain lay elsewhere, the clan chieftains began making new alliances with the priesthood and the imperial court at Kyoto. This led to the destruction of Kamakura and ushered in a period of civil war that lasted for more than three hundred years.

6

The Country at War

THE PERIOD from the close of the fifteenth to the close
of the sixteenth century is known to Japanese historians as *Sengoku Jidai,* the Age of the Country at War.
But there was almost no time before that, from shortly
after the Mongol invasions to 1500, when there was
not fierce fighting in some part of Japan. It was therefore a time of the sword and of the samurai who
wielded the sword.

The Hojo regents had given Japan a hundred
years of law and order and unified it sufficiently to
withstand the Mongol attacks. But when the threat of
invasion was over, their rule came swiftly to an end.
The priests who claimed it was their prayers that had
saved Japan were rewarded. But this left little to give
to the southern chieftans who had done most of the
fighting and nothing for the chieftains who had come

from their lands in the north to aid the men of the south. As a result, dissatisfaction was widespread.

The imperial court at Kyoto tried to take advantage of this general disaffection to regain its lost power, and Emperor Go Daigo led a revolt of armed monks against Kamakura. The Hojo were no longer strong enough to withstand this attack by themselves, so they called on a Minamoto chieftain named Takauji from the northern district of Ashikaga to put down the imperial uprising. But Ashikaga Takauji had his own ideas about where his loyalty lay, and also—as it turned out—about who should rule Japan. Instead of bringing the emperor to heel, he joined forces with him, turned against the Hojo, and on July 5, 1333, Kamakura was captured and burned.

The Emperor Go Daigo now made much the same mistake that the Hojo had made and gave most of the large estates that Takauji and his generals had won, not to them, but to the priests and nobles who surrounded him in court.

Furious, Takauji established headquarters at Kamakura and began ruling that part of the country on his own. When the emperor sent troops against him, he fled to Kyushu, gathered new forces there, and marched on Kyoto where he set up an emperor of his own choosing. Go Daigo, however, escaped from the capital dressed in woman's clothing, taking with him two of the Three Treasures—the Sacred Sword and the Jewel—and set up his court at Yoshino.

Go Daigo's court was known as the Southern Court and that of Takauji's puppet was called the Northern Court. Thus, despite the old Japanese maxim that "just as there is but one sun in heaven, so there is but one emperor on earth," there were now two em-

perors, each claiming to be the rightful one. In 1339
Go Daigo died, the Sacred Treasures were returned to
Kyoto, and Ashikaga Takauji was appointed Shogun
by the emperor of the Northern Court. This did not
end the fighting, however, and the struggle between
the supporters of the two rival courts continued until
1392.

The Ashikaga Shogunate differed from that of
the Hojo in several ways. In the first place, it was the
Shogun himself who now ruled, rather than a regent
who ruled in his name. In the second place, the Ashikaga did not dare leave the capital and base themselves
elsewhere as Yoritomo and the Hojo regents had done,
so they established their court in a district of Kyoto
called Muromachi, though they kept Kamakura as
their military base under a governor general.

The major difference between the Hojo and the
Ashikaga, however, was a result of Takauji's flight to
Kyushu. The Hojo had not been interested in foreign
trade, but the men of Kyushu—living closer to the
mainland than anyone else in Japan—had always
found it very profitable. During his stay there, Takauji
came to see its value also. Trade with China became
one of the chief interests of the Ashikaga Shoguns and
supplied the wealth that enabled them to remain in
power until the middle of the sixteenth century.

It was during this period that the Zen sect of
Buddhists became very important, virtually the official
religion of the samurai class. The Zen priests had re-
tained their contact with China and most of the overseas trade was conducted under their direction which
increased their wealth as well as their power.

The tremendous growth in trade had other significant results. It led to the rise of seaport cities that had

been unimportant towns before; Sakai, for instance, which is now Osaka, was originally merely a place where salt was produced. But with the increase of overseas trade, it became such a rich and busy port that by 1543 the Shoguns were borrowing money from it in exchange for privileges of self-government.

The increase in trade also led to the growth of the merchant class. There had always been trade guilds, but now groups of merchants began putting themselves under the protection of powerful persons or institutions like temples, of course paying for the protection that was given them. These groups were known as *za,* which means a seat. As the merchants grew in strength, they began to take the law into their own hands, establishing monopolies and charging exorbitant prices for even basic commodities such as rice and salt.

But if the merchants were now strong enough to look after their own interests, the peasants were not. Since the economy of the Kamakura administration had been based on the peasants, the Hojo regents had protected them and tried to keep their taxes reasonable. But when the Ashikaga Shoguns began getting most of their wealth from overseas trade, they no longer cared about the peasants and did nothing to help them when feudal landlords and public officials began collecting higher and higher taxes. Finally, especially in times of famine or during epidemics, even the patient and long-suffering peasants began to revolt.

Conditions in Japan grew more and more chaotic. The Shoguns, their supporters, and those involved in the overseas trade grew wealthier. They built lavish pavilions for themselves and indulged in all sorts of extravagances, while the rest of the country grew

poorer and poorer. Just a short distances from the
luxurious court of the Shogun, the emperor lived in a
dilapidated mansion surrounded by nothing but a bamboo fence. Things became so difficult that the Emperor
Go Nara made a living by selling his autograph.
Though he was half-starving, he was still reverenced
as a god and those who wanted an example of his ex-
quisite calligraphy would leave a request for it and
the money to pay for it without daring to look at his
face. And in 1500 the body of Go Tsuchimikado lay
unburied for six weeks because there was no money in
the treasury to pay for his funeral.

It was during this period that Nō plays assumed
a new form, the one that we are familiar with today.
Nō was very old and was originally a form of rhythmic
movement and posturing to the beat of drums and
other instruments. Since it was first performed in the

rice fields, in the beginning it was probably a type of fertility rite similar to the Dionysian rites in Greece that gave rise to the Greek drama. Later on, Nō, which means "ability" or skill," were performed at Shinto shrines and at court during ceremonial occasions, mostly by talented amateurs. Now, however, professional groups developed, special plays were written for the Nō troups; and performances were given for the general public, which had never had an opportunity to see No before.

Nō was one of the few bright notes in a dark era, however. Times of turmoil such as these are always times of opportunity for the ruthless; and clan leaders and feudal lords now began attacking one another, seizing estates where they could. While a code of behavior for the military caste had been worked out during the early days of the Kamakura administration, a code that later came to be called *Bushido* or the Way of the Warrior, there was little evidence of chivalry or loyalty in this period. Might made right, and the only law was the law of the sword.

From the time when the samurai class first developed, when the lord to whom a samurai owed his allegiance died and there was no one to replace him, the samurai lost his rank and became a *ronin* or "wave man," a masterless man without privileges, tossed about like the waves of the sea. But the system also depended on the ability of a lord to reward or punish his followers; and with the anarchy that then prevailed, many lords could no longer support their retainers, and so many samurai now became ronin, though their lords still lived. Those who were willing to take service with another, more fortunate, lord had no difficulty in finding employment in such troubled times. Others drifted into towns or joined the armed forces of monasteries, and still others dropped into the category of *ashigaru* or light foot soldiers, thus helping to form a new class of fighting men, a mercenary group who ranked below the samurai proper.

A general state of warfare continued in one part of Japan or another through most of the fifteenth century, and by 1500 the whole of Japan was at war. With conditions what they were, it is not surprising that when the first contact with the West was made in September, 1542, the thing that interested the Japanese most about the foreign demons was not their great size, blue eyes, or strange coloring, but their firearms.

"It was about two or three feet long, straight, heavy, and hollow," wrote the son of a local chieftain. "One end was closed, and near this end was a small hole through which fire was to be lighted. Some mysterious medicine was put into it with a small round piece of lead and, when one lit the medicine through the hole, the lead piece was discharged and hit everything. Light like lightning was seen and thunder heard; bystanders closed their ears with their hands, and flying birds and running beasts fell before it. One day my father asked the foreigners to teach him its use, and he soon became so skillful that he could nearly hit a white object placed a hundred yards away. He then bought two of these pieces, regardless of the high price asked, and kept them as the most precious treasures of his house."

This first meeting between Japan and the West took place on Tanegashima, an island off Kyushu, when a Chinese junk with three Portuguese aboard landed to escape a typhoon. The Japanese immediately began copying the Portuguese arquebuses, and for centuries afterward the Japanese name for a firearm was *tanegashima*.

It was fortunate that the first contact of the Portuguese with Japan took place near Kyushu, for the men of Kyushu were more interested in trade than any other group in Japan. Their friendly reception brought other Portuguese, and soon all the provinces of the island were competing to attrack them. First, Satsuma seemed to have a monopoly on the traders, then Bungo, and finally Hirado, which remained the center of foreign trade for many years. Firearms continued to be an important item of trade even after the Japanese began manufacturing their own; but in addition the Portuguese brought leather, glassware, woolen cloth and velvet, sugar, and medicine, which they exchanged for gold, silver, and copper.

A few years after Portuguese traders established relations with Japan, Jesuit missionaries arrived. The first of these was Father Francis Xavier, who landed at Satsuma in 1549. Here again the Portuguese were fortunate in that the Japanese associated religion with trade because of the activities of the Zen priests. Though Father Xavier was convinced that the Japanese language had been invented by the devil to make it difficult for him to preach, he had a certain amount of success in making converts in Kyushu, especially since he had a young Japanese with him named Yajiro who had left Japan on one of the first trading ships and become a Christian. Father Xavier remained in Japan for two-and-a-half years, building a few churches and making a very good impression on those feudal chiefs with whom he had audiences. When he left Japan, a young Japanese convert who had adopted the name of Bernard went with him and probably became the first Japanese to be seen in Europe.

Meanwhile, the general disorder had continued throughout Japan. The fact that the early missionaries wrote of many local kings, points to a lack of any centralized authority. But now three men appeared on the scene who were to unify the country and give it the first period of peace it had had in several hundred years.

The first of these was Oda Nobunaga, who was born in 1534, a year after the birth of England's Queen Elizabeth. He was the son of a Taira chieftain of the province of Owari, about halfway between Kyoto and Kamakura. When he was a boy, he was so wild and irresponsible that he was known as *Baka-dono* or Lord Fool; and it was only after his guardian had killed himself in protest at his behavior that he changed his way of life.

When Nobunaga's father died in 1549, the young man inherited the comparatively small family estates and set about increasing them at the expense of neighboring landholders. By 1567, through daring, strategy, marriage, and alliances, he had made himself so powerful that the Emperor Ogimachi appealed to him for aid. Rebellious barons had marched on Kyoto, and the Ashikaga Shogun, Yeshiteru, had taken his own life. His brother, Yoshiaki, who should have succeeded him, had fled. Nobunaga marched on Kyoto, occupied it, and set Yoshiaki up as Shogun. Nobunaga could not become Shogun himself since by precedent only a Minamoto could hold the post; but he was now the most powerful man in the land, exercising that power in the name of the Shogun. And when, some five years later, Yoshiaki began plotting with some of his enemies, Nobunaga deposed him, bringing to an end the

240 years of Ashikaga rule.

Though Nobunaga was now the actual ruler of Japan, issuing decrees in the name of the emperor, he was not without many and powerful enemies. However, he was strongly entrenched in a central location near the capital, which gave him a strategic advantage. And since he was acting as Shogun, theoretically in command of all the armed forces of Japan, anyone who resisted him was technically a rebel, which gave him a moral and psychological advantage. But, perhaps most important, he had the two greatest military men in the country with him, his trusted general, Hideyoshi, and his ally Tokugawa Ieyasu.

Hideyoshi was the son of an ashigaru in the employ of Nobunaga's father; and he was so ugly that as a boy, he was called *Sarumen Kanja* or Monkey Face. Everything seemed to be against him; his personal appearance, his lowly birth, and his lack of education. He had been sent to a Buddhist temple for training when, as a young man, his parents found that they could not handle him. But he had such a violent temper that finally even the Buddhist priests had sent him away. There was only one man in all Japan whom Hideyoshi thought worthy of respect, and that was Nobunaga. He joined his army as a common soldier and fought his way up from the ranks until he had become Nobunaga's right-hand man, his chief adviser in council, and his most reliable general on the battle field.

Ieyasu, the third of the triumvirate, was descended from the Minamoto and got the name Tokugawa from a village in one of the northern provinces where his family had settled. He had been the vassal of one of the chieftains who fought Nobunaga, but when his lord was defeated he went over to Nobunaga's side, married his son to Nobunaga's daughter, and became, along with Hideyoshi, one of his most valuable commanders.

The task the three men faced was formidable, for the chieftains who opposed them were not only each powerful in themselves, but were aided by several of the sects of armed monks. These particular monks were more interested in temporal power than souls, and thus were always willing to fight in support of the local *daimyo,* the important feudal nobles. One by one, Nobunaga defeated his rivals, sometimes by force of arms, sometimes by the treachery that was so common in those days. For example, he lured the monks of Ikko out of their stronghold under a pledge of truce and then massacred them. By 1573 Nobunaga was master of the home provinces, those surrounding Kyoto, and was ready to move on the great chieftains of the mid-lands and the west.

In preparation for this, he built a fortress at Azuchi, about twenty miles northeast of Kyoto. Though the fortress itself was wooden, like all buildings in Japan up to that time, it was set on a massive stone base over seventy feet high. It was the strongest defensive structure in the kingdom, and the first to follow a western model and recognize the fact that warfare had changed with the introduction of firearms some thirty years before. When the fortress was completed, Nobunaga sent Hideyoshi against his most important enemy, Prince Mori of Choshu, whose territory lay in the west. This campaign lasted for five years, unti 1582. When Mori's stronghold was about to fall, Hideyoshi sent for Nobunaga so as to let him take the credit for the victory.

At this moment another of Nobunaga's generals,

Akechi Mitsuhide, turned on his chief. He attacked
Nobunaga as he rested unsuspecting in a temple.
Rather than permit himself to be captured, Nobunaga
killed himself.

Before word of his treacherous act could get to
Hideyoshi, Mitsuhide hurried to Kyoto and forced the
emperor to give him the title of Shogun. He then sent
word to Prince Mori, proposing that they attack Hideyoshi together. But Hideyoshi was as good a statesman
as he was a soldier. He had already arranged a truce
with Mori. Nevertheless, this second bit of treachery
almost succeeded. Hideyoshi was on his way back from
Prince Mori's castle with a small escort when he was
attacked by a large body of horseman, crying, "The

Shogun Mitsuhide has sent us to to take your head!"

Under a cloud of arrows, Hideyoshi turned his horse into a narrow path between the rice fields where his enemies could only follow in single file. There was a temple at the end of the path. Just before he reached it, Hideyoshi jumped from his horse and sent it galloping back along the path, scattering his pursuers. Then he hurred into the shrine where the monks were bathing. He whipped off his clothes, and the monks hid them for him. Quickly they shaved his head and concealed him among them in the heated water. By the time Mitsuhide's horsemen arrived, though he was in plain sight, they could not find him. Shortly afterward, Hideyoshi's bodyguard rode up, and Mitsuhide had lost his chance to dispose of the wily warrior. Gathering his forces, Hideyoshi attacked and defeated Mitsuhide. Twelve days after the death of Nobunaga, the fleeing Shogun was killed by farmers and his head sent to Hideyoshi. His rule was so short that since then he has been known as the Thirteen-days' Shogun.

When the feudal chiefs assembled to choose Nobunaga's successor, Hideyoshi forced the selection of the youngest of the candidates, Nobunaga's grandson, Samboshi. It was thus clear that Hideyoshi, himself, intended to rule.

For a while Hideyoshi was in difficulty because some of his supporters turned against him. There was even conflict between him and Tokuwaga Ieyasu. But finally the two soldiers made peace, and Hideyoshi made their friendship binding by giving Ieyasu his younger sister in marriage.

Though still not complete master of Japan, Hideyoshi was now the strongest man in the kingdom and obviously what he wanted was to be made Shogun.

But such was the strength of precedent that, powerful as he was, he could not be given that title since he was not a Minamoto, was not even of daimyo blood. There were ways around this, of course, since adoption into noble families was not uncommon. The ex-Shogun Yoshiaki could not be persuaded to accept him into the Minamoto family, but the Fujiwara were more amenable. Once he was accepted into that poorer but still aristocratic family, he had himself made *Kwampaku* or Regent.

He now proceeded against his remaining enemies, and by 1590 the last one had surrendered and Japan was at peace for the first time in more than a century.

As soon as Hideyoshi became Regent, he began consolidating his power. He instituted a land survey, which made payment of taxes easier for the peasants than they had been for many years. He conciliated the Buddhist priests and made friends with the nobles. At the same time, he built himself a castle at Osaka that was larger, stronger and far more lavish than the one Nobunaga had built at Azuchi. Finally, he passed a series of edicts that had a profound effect on the samurai.

The introduction of firearms had caused changes in warfare in Japan, modifying strategy and leading to the building of castles like the ones at Azuchi and Osaka. But it had not caused a breakup of the feudal structure, as it did in Europe when the knight on horseback was displaced by the foot soldier, armed first with the longbow and then with the gun. The samurai remained the professional fighting man and, though he now used an arquebus instead of a bow and arrow, his chosen weapon remained the sword. Though Hideyoshi had risen to high estate from an obscure background, once he came to power he seemed determined that there should be no more changes in the social structure. Therefore he enacted laws that forbade a man to leave the station to which he was born, or a samurai to transfer his allegiance from one lord to another.

A year later, in 1587, in order to emphasize the difference between the samurai and the peasants and again make the wearing of a sword a badge of rank, he ordered all peasants to turn in their weapons. This measure, which was known as the Great Sword Hunt, served another purpose, of course, for it removed weapons from the hands of the lower classes who might revolt. Thus, following a long period when the peasants, either from choice or necessity, had taken part in the fighting, the samurai now had the exclusive right to wear a sword. And since at this time, in addition to his long sword or *tachi,* the samurai carried a short one called a *tanto,* he was now known as a "two-sworded man."

By now Hideyoshi had become the *Taiko* or Great Lord, but he was not infallible, and in 1592 he made a serious mistake; he invaded Korea in an attempt to conquer it and then China. There were many reasons for this move. Ambition was one of them. Another was a desire to do something with his huge and efficient armies. He was afraid that if he did not find some fighting for his feudal lords, they might turn on one another or even on him. Whatever the reasons, the move was ill-advised, for the Japanese were short of ships and the Korean navy was large and efficient.

Initially the Japanese forces were successful, driving almost to the Chinese border. But then Chinese troops came to the aid of the Koreans, and the superior

Korean navy cut the Japanese supply lines; so finally and reluctantly, Hideyoshi arranged for a truce.

Five years later he tried again, sending another army to Korea. The struggle went on this time for almost a year. Though the Japanese won many battles, they finally realized that they faced a hopeless task; and when Hideyoshi died in September, 1598, they withdrew.

Under Hideyoshi, many changes had taken place in Japan. Continuing where Nobunaga had left off, the *Taiko* had brought Japan closer to unity than it had been in centuries. And though he was a military man, there were many new developments in art and architecture. An enormous amount of building went on. It was during this time that some of the most beautiful castles in Japan were built, structures with the graceful, many-roofed towers that we now consider typically Japanese.

During this time contact with the Portuguese had its effect, too. It became fashionable for young courtiers to wear high-crowned hats, cloaks, and full trousers like the foreign traders. Though the Portuguese influence on dress was limited and short-lived, evidences of their presence can still be seen in the Japanese language. Since it was the Portuguese who introduced playing cards into Japan, the Japanese still call them *karuta,* after the Portuguese *carta.* One of the most curious transformations, however, came about because the Portuguese, as good Catholics, would not eat meat on Ember Days which they called *Quattuor Tempora,* (*Four times*—for the four times a year these special holy days occur.) And since they would eat only seafood then and preferred it fried, we now find *tempura* on Japanese menus, the Latin word for *times* having turned into seafood fried in batter.

Before he died, Hideyoshi had set up a council to look after the interests of his young son, Hideyori. Ieyasu, as the lord of eight provinces in the northeast, was easily the most powerful man on the council and, like Nobunaga and Hideyoshi before him, was concerned primarily with his own interests. He began strengthening his position by marrying his many sons and daughters to feudal lords in different parts of Japan. When the other members of the council, particularly those in the south, realized what he was up to, civil war broke out. But this conflict was short-lived. In October, 1600, Ieyasu led his forces against an army that was almost twice as large and defeated it decisively at Sekigahara, not far from the capital.

A patient and farseeing man, Ieyasu took no further action against Hideyori for the time being, but used the spoils won at Sekigahara to further consolidate his power. Since he was a Minamoto, in 1603 the emperor gave him the title of Shogun.

Though he was now legitimately the ruler of Japan, Ieyasu continued to move carefully. Hideyori was now twelve years old and still had many strong supporters. In order to have them think that he was holding the power in trust until Hideyori came of age, Ieyasu married the boy to his granddaughter. At the same time he now made Yedo, some twenty miles northeast of Kamakura, his military and administrative capital. He did this for the same reason that Yoritomo had established his capital in that area; to rule from the center of his military power and to keep his followers from the intrigues and corruption of court life in Kyoto. But he also intended to make Yedo the cultural and economic center of Japan, and he succeeded in this as he did in everything else he attempted, for Yedo is now known as Tokyo.

When Ieyasu first established himself at Yedo, it was a small village in a swamp. But he called on the daimyo in various parts of the country to help build the new city; and soon the whole country was involved, digging canals, filling the marshes, and building roads and bridges. This served two purposes, for it not only created the new city he wanted, but it kept the feudal lords so busy that they could not plot against him.

Once the city was established, he set up new and efficient administrative machinery and further strengthened his position by dealing generously with the Buddhists and the court at Kyoto. He gave the emperor more than eight times the amount of taxes that Hideyoshi had allowed him.

The course of Christianity in Japan had been very uneven since the landing of Francis Xavier some fifty-odd years before. The Jesuits had been very successful under Nobunaga; and, under Hideyoshi, Spanish missionaries of the Franciscan order came to Japan from Manila. When a Spanish captain, hoping to intimidate Hideyoshi, told him that wherever missionaries went, troops followed, Hideyoshi was enraged and ordered the missionaries to be put to death. Some thirty of them were crucified at Nagasaki, and others left the country; but over a hundred remained to continue their work secretly.

Generally speaking, Ieyasu was tolerant of the Christians and favored them in accordance with the amount of trade they brought. However, in 1600 a man arrived in Japan who was at least partly responsible for a change in the Shogun's attitude toward the missionaries. He was an Englishman named Will

Adams. He was a true Elizabethan sea dog, a captain who had helped fight the Spanish Armada under Drake. In 1598 he had taken service with the Dutch as pilot major of a fleet of five ships on a trading venture to the Far East. His ship, the *Charity,* had become separated from the others and landed at Bungo on Kyushu.

Though the Dutch had already begun to do some trading with Japan, Adams was the first Englishman to reach the country and was brought before Ieyasu. When the Shogun asked him if his country had wars, Adams said, "Yes, with the Spanish and Portugals, being in peace with all other nations."

The Portuguese missionaries and merchants tried to tell Ieyasu that Adams, like all Englishmen, was a bad and dangerous man, but the Shogun was much taken with him. He made Adams his adviser on foreign affairs and on shipbuilding. One of the ships Adams designed and built was loaned to a Spanish ambassador and, with a Japanese crew aboard, sailed to the Spanish colony in California some ten years before the Pilgrims landed at Plymouth Rock.

Ieyasu gave Adams honors, land, and a Japanese wife, and considered him too important and valuable to let him return to England. Adams of course did not like the Spanish and Portuguese. Under his influence Ieyasu realized that it was possible to have foreign trade without foreign priests. With this, his attitude towards the missionaries began to change, and he issued edicts banning Christianity and ordering all missionaries to leave the country.

The Christians were very strong in the southwest, however, and at first Ieyasu's orders were not obeyed. Instead several priests went to Osaka and asked Hideyoshi's son, Hideyori, for aid. Ieyasu realized then that he must settle the matter of the succession once and for all. He besieged Hideyori's castle with an army of one hundred and fifty thousand men armed with English and Dutch cannon and muskets; but Hideyoshi had built well, and it was impossible to take the castle. After several weeks of vain assaults, Ieyasu offered a truce on only one condition; that part of the outer wall be torn down and the moat filled in. He only wanted this done to save face, he explained, for it would not do for him to have failed completely in his attempt. Somewhat reluctantly, Hideyori agreed, and his reluctance was justified. The following summer Ieyasu attacked again and, after stubborn fighting, was able to penetrate the breached walls and take the castle. Rather than submit to capture, Hideyori killed himself.

Ieyasu was now the unchallenged ruler of Japan. Some years before, he had made his son, Hidetata, the Shogun, but of course he continued to order the affairs of the empire himself. There were now about two hundred feudal lords in Japan, some two million samurai, and between twenty-five and thirty million common people. Ieyasu had already made a distinction between the lords who had supported him before Sekigahara, who were known as *Fudai* or hereditary vassals, and those who had submitted to him afterwards and were called *Tozama* or outside vassals. Now he extended the distinctions, dividing the commoners into farmers, artists and artisans, and merchants. These distinctions became absolutely rigid with no marriage permitted between the different classes and no possibility of moving up from one class to the next. Further laws regulated all the activities of the various classes, not only giving them codes of conduct, but prescribing their clothes and specifying what kinds of houses they could build, what kinds of weddings they could have, and what kinds of gifts they could give.

In 1616 Ieyasu died; but he had built far better than either Nobunaga or Hideyoshi, and the Tokugawa Shogunate continued to rule Japan for more than two hundred and fifty years afterward. In comparing the three men, it has been said that Nobunaga quarried the stones for the new Japan, that Hideyoshi rough-cut them, and that Ieyasu fitted them into place. Ieyasu was able to complete the unification of Japan only because he followed two other remarkable men. Though all three were alike in some respects, they were quite different in others, particularly in temperament. Their differences are summed up in three *haiku,* the short Japanese poems, supposedly describing their attitudes while waiting for the first cuckoo to sing in the spring. Nobunaga's poem goes:

> *The cuckoo:*
> *If it does not sing,*
> *I its neck will surely wring.*

Hideyoshi's goes:

> *The cuckoo:*
> *If it does not sing,*
> *I will teach the stubborn thing.*

And Ieyasu's:

> *The cuckoo:*
> *If to sing it's not inclined,*
> *In time it's bound to change its mind.*

After Ieyasu's death, harsher measures were taken against the Christians; and again all missionaries were ordered to leave the country. Those who did not were killed and so were many of the Japanese converts who insisted on practising their new faith. Persecution could not suppress belief, but it did provoke violence. In 1637 there was a revolt of Japanese converts in the Shimabara district of Kyushu. An army was sent against them, but thirty thousand of them—men, women and children—held out in a castle they had seized for more than two months. When the castle finally fell, only a handful was spared; all the rest were massacred.

Convinced that foreign influence was responsible for the revolt, the Shogun Iyemitsu barred all traders except the Dutch, and confined them to a small island in the harbor of Nagasaki. His edict said, "Let none, so long as the Sun illuminates the world, presume to sail to Japan, not even in the quality of ambassadors, and this declaration is never to be revoked on pain of death."

Japan had decided to cut herself off from the rest of the world. Amaterasu had once again withdrawn into her cave, and the West was not to see her face again for more than two hundred years.

III

*The Treasures
and the
Samurai*

鎌倉時代

7

The Mirror

WHEN Amaterasu, the Sun Goddess, first hid herself in the cave, it was the Sacred Mirror that restored her to mankind. Hearing the laughter of the other gods, she peered out. But it was only when she caught sight of herself in the Mirror, that she actually left the cave. Later, when she gave the Mirror, along with the Sword and the Jewel, to her grandson, Ninigi, she said: "When thou lookest upon this mirror, my child, let it be as though thou wert looking on me. Let it be with thee on thy couch and in thy hall. Let it be to thee a holy mirror."

Amaterasu's Mirror was, and still is, kept at Ise, Japan's most sacred shrine. But almost all the Shinto shrines have similar mirrors: polished discs of metal placed so that worshippers cannot avoid looking into them. There is no vanity in this. It is, in fact, just the opposite. For just as the essence of Greek wisdom can be found in the inscription on the Temple of Apollo in Delphi which says, "Know Thyself," so the sacred mirrors of Japan say: "To know others, you must first know yourself. Look here and see what you find of beauty and ugliness, of good and evil."

The Mirror, as an image of the self, is a reflection of Japanese religious beliefs.

The earliest Japanese religion—even before the arrival of Amaterasu—was one in which natural elements were deified; not only the sun, moon, and storms, but mountains, rivers and trees as well. When invaders came to Japan from the mainland, they undoubtedly brought Amaterasu with them, and she became the leading deity. Her shrine was probably established at Ise because it was already a sacred place in the earlier religion.

One of the important elements in the Japanese religion—and one that plays an important part in the Japanese character even today—is the fact that it was based on an appreciation of nature rather than on fear. Though their country is often shaken by earthquakes and swept by storms and floods, the early Japanese had no evil earthquake god, and even their storm god generally appeared only in his kindly aspect. This is probably because the invaders came to Japan from the arid regions of Korea and north China or the chill and windy plains of Siberia. The comparatively gentle climate of Japan, its fertile soil and many rivers and trees, probably made such an impression on them that they could only respond with gratitude. Certainly their early religion, which was later called Shinto, was one of love and gratitude rather than fear; and the purpose of its rites was to praise and thank their deities rather than to placate them with sacrifices.

In the early times the clan chieftains acted as priests, performing the religious ceremonies for the entire clan. The chief of the imperial clan, the emperor, acted as high priest as well as ruler. The earliest Japanese word for government is *matsurigoto*, which means religious observances. But even in these times there were special groups who performed special religious functions: the *Imibe*, for instance, whose duty it was to insure the ritual purity of everyone and everything connected with the religious rites; the Nakatomi clan who recited the prayers and communicated with the gods on behalf of the emperor; and the *Urabe* or diviners who interpreted the will of the gods by examining the burned shoulder blade of a deer or by other prescribed methods.

One of the outstanding features of Shinto was the great accent that was placed on ritual purity. The Imibe were men whose chief duty was to keep themselves free of all forms of pollution so that they could approach the gods without offense. Personal cleanliness was, of course, basic, and bathing and putting on fresh garments was a necessary preparation for any religious observance. Since Shinto was not based on a moral or ethical code, most of the forms of impurity that were to be avoided were physical. Disease and wounds, for example, were forms of uncleanliness. But the greatest of all sources of contamination was death. This is why, until the beginning of the eighth century, the capital— or at least the imperial palace—was moved to another location after the death of each emperor.

The most significant of the Shinto rites, the *O-harai* or Great Purification, took place twice a year, in June and December. At these times the people rid themselves of all their sins and pollutions by transferring them to pieces of paper cut in the shape of human beings which were then thrown into the rivers or into the sea. This rite is similar to the ancient Hebrew rite of the scapegoat, where a goat was driven into the wilderness to carry away the sins of the congregation.

But although one of the chief features of Shinto was its accent on purity, its major objective was fertility. Its most important ceremonies have to do in one way or another with the production food. The chief festivals of the year are the Tasting of the First Fruits, the Divine Tasting, and the Together Tasting, in which the emperor joins the gods in partaking of the season's new rice and rice wine. The most solemn festival of all is the Great Food Offering, an elaborate form of the festival of the First Fruits. It is celebrated only when a new emperor mounts the throne.

In the very early days, rocks and springs were worshipped out-of-doors, and prayers were made to the sun itself. Later, ceremonies were conducted within an enclosure marked off by the branches of evergreen trees thrust into the ground. It was only when jewels and mirrors began to symbolize a god that shrines were needed. The word for shrine, *miya,* comes from the word *ya,* meaning "house," with the honorific prefix *mi*. The same word is used for a chief's house. This would indicate that originally there was no distinction between an ordinary house and a shrine. One of the characteristics of the Shinto shrine is its simplicity. The shrines at Ise, which are pulled down and rebuilt in exactly the same form every twenty years, represent the purest and most ancient style of Japanese architecture. They are still modelled on the old shrines which were little more than thatched huts.

The congregation does not enter the shrine to worship, so only enough space is required for the altar and the priests. Worship consisted of obeisance, prayer, and offerings; the offerings being primarily food and drink. Later, cloth was added, and eventually a symbolic offering came into use in which strips of paper, representing cloth, were fastened to a stick and placed on the altar. Private worship was very uncommon. Most of the rites were conducted by the emperor or the priests for all the people. When there was any private worship, it consisted of placing an offering on the shrine and making a reverent gesture such as bowing or clapping.

Buddhism was first introduced in Japan from Korea in the middle of the sixth century. By that time it was already almost a thousand years old. The founder of Buddhism was Prince Siddhartha who was born about 568 B.C. in northeastern India near the border of Nepal. His father was chief of the Sakya tribe. Though brought up in luxury, when he was about thirty he became filled with a sense of the misery and impermanence of life and left his wife and son to search for the ultimate truth. He first looked for it among the Brahman ascetics of Benares, but their teachings did not satisfy him. So he began solitary meditation under a Bo tree, a place which remains sacred to the Buddhists to this day.

As a result of his meditations, Siddhartha attained illumination or true comprehension and became The Buddha, that is, one who had attained true knowledge. He then set forth to preach his doctrine of the Four Noble Truths, which are: all men suffer; the cause of suffering is desire; the cure for suffering is the elimination of desire; and the way to eliminate desire is to follow the Eightfold Path which consists of: right belief, right intention, right speech, right behavior, right occupation, right effort, right meditation, and right concentration.

Buddha taught that all living things, plants and animals as well as men, want a higher life and will finally achieve it. But it takes a long time to do this; one lifetime is never enough. In a sense, Buddha was teaching what the Indian people had long believed: that after death a person is born again in another body and goes on being born again and again until he is wise and pure enough to achieve the supreme good, Nirvana. If he lives one life badly, he will have to pay for it in the next. But if he lives well, he will be born in a higher state the next time, for life follows eternal laws and a man will reap as he has sown.

While Buddhism had many similarities to Brahmanism, it differed from it in its spirit of universal charity and sympathy. As a result, it began to spread rapidly through India and into China. Soon two different systems of Buddhism developed: *Hinayana* or the "Little Vehicle," and *Mahayana* or the "Great Vehicle." Hinayana, the chief Indian type, was atheistic. Since Buddha himself had been a man, the followers of this system believed that everyone must achieve salvation by himself. Mahayana, the type that eventually reached Japan by way of China, believed that Buddha, while not actually a god, could be worshipped in a number of forms. They felt that man could be saved through the efforts of the Bodhisattvas or future Buddhas.

In China the new faith was soon accepted along with Confucianism and Taoism, which were primarily moral codes, and became one of the Three Religions.

By the time Buddhism reached Japan, it had changed greatly from the simplicity of the early teachings of Buddha. For when the King of Paikché in Korea sent the Japanese Emperor Kimmei a gold and copper statue of Buddha in the middle of the sixth century, it was accompanied by monks and many books of prayers. The message recommending the new religion said that, though it was difficult to explain and understand, it was the best of all faiths.

It was at this time that the great struggle took place in Japan between the Soga family, who saw in the new religion a means of attaining power, and the Nakatomi, who were the hereditary priests of the existing religion. It was also at this time that the old religion began to be called Shinto, no name having been necessary before this since there was no other, competing religion.

From this time on, Buddhism spread rapidly, though Shintoism continued and still continues to be practised. For while Buddhism is a personal religion, practised by individuals, Shintoism was and is conducted principally by the emperor and a group of priests on behalf of the country as a whole.

Buddhism soon began to assume new and purely Japanese forms and also to include some elements of Shintoism. One example of this came in the Nara period when the Buddhist priests brought the old sea-god Yawata from Kyushu, where he had long been worshipped, not only as a god of the sea, but also as the god of wars and victories. The name Yawata means Eight Banners. But when they enshrined him at the capital, they changed the reading of his name to Hachiman and said that the eight banners stood for the eight right ways of Buddha.

In the early days, the practice of Buddhism was more magical than religious. *Sutras* or prayers like the Lotus or the Diamond Cutter were recited to avert disaster or secure good fortune. By the Nara period, however, understanding had increased and six major sects had developed. They all attempted to rid man of the illusions of the senses so that he could discover the truth that was the real meaning of the universe. This, they believed, was the only way to attain salvation. The differences between them were chiefly differences in the way they believed this could be achieved.

It was during this period that Buddhist temples became large institutions, spreading over several acres and enclosed by high walls. The entrance was always an ornamental gate on the south side of the enclosure, and in the center was the Golden Hall where the statue of Buddha was enshrined. The Golden Hall, was not

very large. But, since it was the heart of the temple, it was as beautiful as the priests and worshippers could make it. The statue of Buddha, often gilded, was surrounded by wall paintings and ceremonial banners of richly colored silk. Thus the introduction of Buddhism had an important and continuing effect on Japanese art.

Buddhism continued to grow and develop, and though some of the sects of the Nara period eventually disappeared, other new ones evolved. One of these was the Tendai sect which took its name from a Chinese monastery on Mount T'ien-t'ai. Its central belief was that all phenomena are actually one, that the whole universe is a manifestation of Buddha, and that even a grain of sand includes some of his spiritual nature. It believed that enlightenment did not come from meditation or good works or wisdom alone, but from a combination of all three.

At about the same time, another sect known as Shingon or True Word was introduced from China. Its basic beliefs were similar to Tendai, but its position was that its doctrines could not be explained in words. The believer, however, could be helped to enlightenment by talismans.

There is a moving letter from Saicho, founder of the Tendai sect, to one of his disciples who deserted him for the Shingon sect in which he said:

"We were baptised together. In company we have sought for Truth, in unison we have hoped for Grace. Why now have you turned your back upon the Original Vow and left me for so long? It is the way of the world to reject the worse and take the better, but how can there be a worse or better as between the doctrine of Tendai and the doctrine of Shingon? For good friends,

Truth is one and Love is one . . ."

But the disciple replied that there was a difference between the two doctrines and, begging his master's forgiveness, said he must remain with the Shingon sect.

In later years, after the death of Saicho, the Tendai sect became more interested in worldly possessions and power than spiritual matters. Their monastery at Hieizan became a breeding ground for the type of militant warrior-priests who afterwards gave Nobunaga, Hideyoshi, and Ieyasu so much trouble.

As the number of sects increased and their doctrines became more and more complicated, it was inevitable that there should be a move back to simplicity. This came at the end of the tenth century with the teaching of a priest of the Tendai sect named Genshin. His doctrine was named *Amidism* after the aspect of Buddha that was called Amida, the Lord of Boundless Light. Genshin taught that Amida Buddha had refused to accept enlightenment himself unless he could be sure that all living things could be saved by faith in him. Therefore faith was sufficient for salvation, and the believer had only to invoke the name of Amida Buddha and he would be born again in *Jodo*, the Pure Land.

This doctrine did away with the complicated theology and ritual of the other sects, and more and more of the faithful began the practice of *nembutsu*, the repetition of the phrase, *Namu Amida Butsu*, "Merciful Buddha, hear my prayer," which would take away their sins and redeem them. This sect later developed into the Jodo sect which is one of the largest in Japan today.

In contrast to the Jodo sect was the *Hokke* or Lotus sect, founded during the Kamakura period by Nichiren, one of the greatest figures in Japanese religious history. Nichiren was a revivalist as well as a reformer, preaching in the streets. Since this was at the time when Japan was threatened by the Mongol invasions, he won many followers. The essence of his teaching was the need for a return to the early purity of Tendai Buddhism.

But of all the Buddhist sects the one that had the greatest influence on the culture of Japan, and the one that is best known today in the West, is Zen.

The word *Zen* comes, through the Chinese, from the Sanskrit *dhyana*, and means meditation. It is said to have begun with the arrival of an Indian monk named Bodhidharma in China in the year 520. While many of its doctrines were known in Japan during the Nara period, its real development came during the Kamakura period, about the year 1200. At that time a monk, Eisai, returned to Japan after having been converted to Zen during a stay in China.

Zen differed from others forms of Buddhism in several important ways. Most of the Buddhist sects taught an acceptance of life in all its aspects, the bad as well as the good. The Jodo sect taught that after death came a rebirth. But Zen went even further, teaching that good without evil is like up without down, and that therefore life and death were merely different aspects of the same thing. The goal of Zen is to learn one's true nature and attain Buddhahood; this cannot be achieved through study or even instruction, but only through meditation. A Zen teacher does not read *sutras*, worship an image, or perform any ceremonies. He teaches only by vague hints and parodoxical answers to questions which are in a sense riddles, called *koan*. For instance, an early Chinese disciple came to his master and asked, "What is the method of liberation?"

"Who binds you?" asked his master.

"No one binds me."

"Why then should you seek liberation?" asked the master.

A typical first koan is for a student to be told to discover his "original face," in other words his original nature, as it was before he was born. He is told to return when he has discovered it and give some proof of his discovery. Meanwhile he is taught how to sit, usually facing a blank wall, while meditating and keeping his mind empty. Even when he is not meditating the student of Zen leads a difficult life, eating and sleeping at odd hours and working at menial and physical tasks. Eventually, if he is fortunate, after he has given his master many answers to this first koan and to others, and after he has been rebuffed, contradicted and even struck, he achieves that sudden enlightenment which is called *satori*. This is a revelation or understanding of the truth that comes as suddenly as a flash of lightning. The basic technique of Zen, therefore, is for the student to examine and master himself and find his true place in the universe through his own efforts.

This form of Buddhism that did not necessarily require the study of scriptures and had no complicated philosophy appealed to realistic feudal warriors like the samurai. It was not something that was separate from life, but was very much a part of it. Even today when Westerners wish to study Zen under a Zen master, they find they cannot study it by itself, but only along with something else. For instance, when the German philosopher, Eugen Herrigel, approached a Zen teacher, he was given a choice of instruction in either archery or swordsmanship. He chose archery and later wrote his famous book, *Zen in the Art of Archery*. His wife studied Zen through instruction in flower arrangement.

In addition to the simplicity of its doctrine and its insistence that enlightenment comes suddenly and through a man's own efforts, Zen also taught self-discipline and self-reliance. Its technique enabled a man to study his own nature and arrive at an understanding of the fact that all things were actually one. Once he had arrived at this understanding, he could endure pain and face death with complete calm. A state of mind such as this was very important to a warrior.

The simplicity of Zen Buddhism and its teachings did not appeal only to the samurai, but had a great effect on all forms of Japanese culture. Zen artists did not paint with the bright colors and elaborate detail of some of the earlier schools, but achieved their effects with black ink and as few brush strokes as possible. In Zen architecture, the accent was on proportion rather

than on intricate carving, gilding, or other forms of decoration. A structure that was built under Zen influence seems part of its surroundings. Landscaping was always included in the general plan, and care was taken to keep the gardens and everything around the building as natural as possible.

Though some of the Zen doctrine may seem difficult to understand, not all of it is so different from western thinking. For instance, it was the custom of a professor of semantics at a midwestern American university to hold up a match-box and say, "What is this?"

"A matchbox," some student would reply.

"Is it? *Matchbox* is a series of vowels and consonants, a noise. Is *this* a noise?" and he would throw the matchbox at the student.

In other words, while we may describe an object in words, the words are not, and cannot be, the object itself.

As for the concept of oneness, modern psychiatry talks about this also. According to psychiatry, when a baby is born he *is* without being aware that he is. At a somewhat later stage he becomes aware that he is, but has no consciousness that he is not *all* that is, that anything else exists besides and apart from himself. It is only when he begins to realize that there are other things and people in the world and that he is separate from them that he begins to develop as a person. It is possible that it is this early sense of oneness with everything in the universe, something we all had once and then lost, that the practitioners of Zen strive for.

Finally, we have the insistence of the Zen masters that their teachings should be learned by a study of the self. This can be somewhat explained by examining the Heisenberg Principle of Indeterminacy, a concept in modern physics. It maintains that we can never measure anything really accurately for, in measuring it, we change it somewhat. While we are measuring the air pressure in a tire with a gauge, we are letting a little of the air out of the tire and thus changing the pressure slightly. When we measure the temperature of the water in a bath with a thermometer, the thermometer absorbs some of the heat and changes the temperature somewhat. The chief use of this theory is in the measurement of quantities and objects that are infinitely small, as in nuclear physics. But it is possible that it is for somewhat similar reasons that Zen teachers refuse to explain their doctrine. It may be that they feel that in the very act of explaining what they believe to a student, they will be changing him in a way that would make it impossible for him to learn the truth in as simple, direct, and pure a form as he would if he discovered it for himself.

Whether any explanation of Zen can ever approach its true nature is, of course, open to question. The Western scholar tries. But the Japanese Zen masters say:

> *"Those who know do not speak;*
> *Those who speak do not know."*

8

The Sword

THE SECOND of the Three Treasures of Japan is the Sword.

"There is no country in the world where the sword has received so much honor and renown as in Japan," said Thomas McClatchie, a nineteenth century authority on Japan. "Regarded as of divine origin, dear to the general as a symbol of authority, cherished by the samurai as a part of himself, considered by the common people as their protection against violence, how can we wonder to find it called the living soul of the samurai?"

This expression of the attitude of the Japanese toward the sword is clearly shown in the *Heike Monogatari*, an epic written during the Kamakura period, which opens with a chapter called the *Book of the Sword*.

"Haiku received the sword Zoku-so of Kibu and therewith slew the white serpent and gained the imperial throne," it begins. "Shi-Ko took the dirk of Kei-Ka and with it slew the emissary of Yen, thereby fulfilling a brilliant destiny and laying the foundations of a lasting sway. The authority of the White Standard and the Golden Axe, the might of bow and arrow, horse and stone, the Five Rules of Strategy and the Four Kinds of Benevolence are the methods of ruling a country. But swords are the weapons of highest praise.

"Now in Nippon there are many famous swords. There are the Sacred Swords: *Totsuka-No-Tsurugi*, the Ten-handbreadth Sword; *Hige-kiri*, the Beard-cutter; *Hiza-kiri*, Knee-cutter; and *Kogarasu Maru*, Little Crow."

The Ten-handbreadth Sword was the Sword of the Clustering Clouds of Heaven that was given to Ninigi by the goddess Amaterasu and was later called *Kusanagi* or Grass-cutter.

The oldest swords that have been found in Japan are bronze. The earliest iron swords date from about the beginning of the Christian era and were probably brought in by one of the early migrations from the mainland. These swords were two-and-a-half to three feet long, straight and double-edged. They were very heavy and were called *ken*. The scabbards were generally made of wood, bound with metal bands, and the guards were pierced with holes to make them lighter. *Kusanagi*, the Sacred Sword, was of this type. Even when the early swordsmiths began tempering the iron and making swords of steel, the tempering was faulty; and until about 800 or 900 A.D. the sword was not considered as important a weapon as the bow.

The first Japanese swordsmith whose name we

know was Amakuni, who probably lived in the Uda district of Yamato about the year 700. However, the ancient writings also mention an Amakuni. They say that Sujin, the emperor who ruled during the early part of the third century, was afraid to dwell in the same place as the Sacred Sword, *Kusanagi*, since "It had no equal in this country and being the gigantic weapon that watches over it, it is a thing to dread and of which one should not even speak." So he had a swordsmith named Amakuni make a copy of the sword. This was then kept at the palace and the Sacred Sword itself was removed to the shrine at Atsuta. While it is possible that there was an earlier swordsmith named Amakuni, it is more likely that the name of the earlier smith was lost and that he was given the name of the oldest known swordsmith.

The historic swordsmith Amakuni was apparently the head of a group of smiths who made weapons for the Emperor Mommu and his warriors around the beginning of the eighth century. Legend has it that Amakuni and his son, Amakura, were standing outside their workshop after an important battle, waiting for the emperor and his fighting men to return. The emperor passed by without so much as a glance at the smith. Realizing that this was a rebuke, Amakuni looked more closely at the warriors' weapons and saw that more than half of them were carrying broken swords.

He and his son began collecting the broken swords and examining them. It was obvious that there was something wrong with the way they had been forged. Remembering the emperor's silent rebuke, Amakuni said, "With the aid of the gods, I will make a sword that will not break!"

He and his son shut themselves in their forge and prayed for seven days and seven nights. Then, selecting the iron ore with great care, they refined it and began attempting to make a blade that would fulfill their vow. They worked for thirty days. Finally, gaunt and exhausted, they came out of the shop with a blade that had a single edge and was not straight but slightly curved. Though the other swordsmiths thought them mad, Amakuni and his son began grinding and polishing this new type of blade.

During the months that followed Amakuni and his son continued to turn out this new type of sword. The following spring the emperor and his men went off to battle again, carrying the new swords. Even more anxiously now, Amakuni and his son waited for the warriors to return. When they did, Amakuni began counting the swords—ten, twenty, thirty—every one of the new swords had stood the test of battle! The emperor appeared, smiled at Amakuni and said, "You are the greatest of swordmakers. Not one of your swords has failed us."

With a full heart, Amakuni gave thanks to the gods for having helped him fulfill his vow.

Whether this legend, told by the smiths of Yamato province, is true or not, this new type of sword—called the *katana*—seems to have made its first appearance about the year 900. The katana differed from the ken in several important ways. It was single-edged rather than double-edged; it was not straight but curved, with its edge, faceline, and back all parallel; and while its edge was highly tempered so it would cut, the back was tempered differently so it would be resilient and the blade would not break.

The process of making one of these noble blades

was a long and painstaking one and was approached
with a spirit of reverence. Even today, before a sword
of the old type is forged, the smith undergoes ritual
purification and prays. While he is at work, he wears
white priestly robes. Although it is wood, fire, water,
metal and earth that are used in making the blade, the
Japanese believe that something of the spirit enters
into it, too, and thus each blade has its own character.

This first step in making a sword was the refining
of the iron ore. Though Japan does not have vast natural resources, she does have magnetic iron ore similar
to that used in the famous Swedish steel. This is the
type generally used. After the ore was refined, several
strips of metal were welded together to make a bar
about six inches long, two inches wide, and half an inch
thick. This was heated, folded back upon itself, and
forged again to its original size. This was repeated from
twelve to eighteen times. Several bars like this were
forged and welded together, and then the entire mass
was folded and forged before it was beaten out into a
blade.

The ancient smiths would often chant while they worked. It is said that Masamune, one of the greatest of the swordsmiths who flourished in the latter part of the Kamakura period, set the rhythm for his hammering with the phrase, *"Tenka taihei!"*, "Peace on earth." But Muramasa, his most famous disciple, used to chant, *"Tenka tairan!"*, "War on earth." Possibly as a result of this, it was claimed that once one of Muramasa's blades was drawn, it could not be sheathed again until it had shed blood.

It is also said that one day a warrior, wishing to test a Muramasa blade, set it in a stream and found that every leaf that was carried against the edge by the current was cut in half. But when he placed a Masamune blade in the stream, he found that the leaves avoided the blade. Thus, while both blades had magnificent edges, the Muramasa could not go beyond cutting, but the Masamune would not cut unless it was necessary. A Muramasa blade was terrible, but there was something inspiring about a Masamune blade.

The next step in the making of the sword was the tempering. The whole blade was covered with a composition of clay and other materials. Then the portion that covered the edge was removed with a bamboo stick. The clay covered blade was heated in charcoal until it had reached the proper heat, the back glowing red and the exposed edge white. It was then removed from the fire and quenched in water of the proper temperature. In this process the edge developed an extremely hard crystalline structure called *martensite,* while the rest of the blade remained softer and more flexible. At the same time the upper portion of the highly tempered section showed an irregular line where the clay remained. This varied in the work of different smiths and helped identify the maker.

The early swordsmiths attempted to preserve the secrets of their art and, since they had no way of measuring temperature, they would pass on their knowledge to their sons or trusted disciples in such phrases as: "Heat the steel at the final forging until it is the color of the moon when it rises on a June evening." or "After the final forging, place the sword in water that has the temperature of a stream in February."

One famous swordsmith was called the Master of the One Hand. It is said that he got his name because, when he was an apprentice, he had learned all the arts of swordmaking except the temperature of the water to be used at the final tempering. He was always sent out of the shop during the process, but one day he came bursting in and thrust his hand into the water. Seizing a finished sword, his master cut off his hand. Whether this story is true or not, it underlines the way in which the smiths guarded the secrets of swordmaking.

After the tempering came the sharpening and polishing. It took years to learn to sharpen and polish a sword blade, and the sword polisher was almost as highly honored as the smith. Working with six or seven different grades of whetstones, the polisher would first sharpen the blade on two different planes—the edge plane and the body plane—and then polish it, a process that might take several weeks. If the blade was polished too much, it would shine like a mirror. This was considered too gentle and monotonous. On the other hand, if it was not polished sufficiently and the grain of the metal could be seen distinctly, the blade was considered coarse.

A perfect sword blade had a surface that was serene and deep, with three different hues or gleams; it was highly polished and shining near the ridge and back; grayish white at the edge; and milky on the border between the two.

Before a swordsmith turned a blade over to a polisher, he engraved his signature on the tang, the upper portion of the blade that fitted inside the handle. Sometimes he would also engrave a motto or a verse on it, such as: "There is naught between heaven and earth that a man who carries this blade need fear." or "One's fate is in the hands of heaven, but a skillful fighter does not meet with death." or "In one's last days, one's sword becomes the wealth of one's posterity."

While the swordsmith and polisher were working on the blade itself, other artists—and they were artists —were making the mountings: the hilt and hilt ornaments; the handle bindings; the guard and the sheath. Each of these has a name. The guard, intricately carved and often inlaid with gold, is called the *tsuba*. The small ornaments in various shapes that are bound to the sharkskin covering of the hilt with silk cords are called *menuki*. It was because the menuki were carved in the form of young crows on one of the famous swords of the Minamoto that it was called *Kogarasu Maru* or Baby Crow. And it was because of the artistry that went into the detailed work of the sword mountings that they have been called the jewelry of the samurai.

Since the sword made by a famous smith had enormous value, smiths who were not so well-known would sometimes put a master's name on one of their own swords. It is said that one day Kanemitsu, a famous smith in Bizen province, was resting in his shop when he heard the sound of a chisel in a neighboring shop. Hurrying in there, he seized the blade on which his neighbor had been incising an inscription.

"How dare you do that?" said Kanemitsu angrily. "You were putting my name on that sword, weren't you?"

"Yes," admitted the smith. "But how did you know? Were you watching?"

"No," said Kanemitsu, "but I was listening and you used more strokes than you would have had to if you had been writing your own name."

Though katana are all alike in that they are single-edged and curved, they are classified into different types according to length and the way they were worn. The oldest form of katana was quite long with a four and sometimes even five-foot blade. It was worn slung from the hip by two cords and it is called a *tachi*. It was accompanied by a sword less than a foot in length that was thrust through the sash and called a *tanto*. Later, fashions in swords changed and long swords were made with shorter blades, between two and three feet in length. These are called *daito* and were accompanied by a sword between one and two feet in length called a *wakizashi*. Both of these were worn thrust through the sash. Since the samurai always carried at least two swords, he sometimes referred to them as the great and the small—*dai-sho*.

Once the katana was developed, the sword became the favorite weapon of the samurai and was worn by them until well past the middle of the nineteenth century. And with the almost constant warfare that began during the latter half of the Heian period, the need for swords constantly increased and so did the number of swordsmiths. The most famous smiths appeared between the years 900 and 1450. The greatest of these are generally considered to be Munechika, who lived during the tenth century, Masamune, who came at the end of the thirteenth century, and Yoshimitsu and Muramasa, who both lived and worked during the fourteenth century. The techniques of each of these and of all other smiths differed somewhat, as a result, the swords that they made all differed to a greater or lesser degree in length, curvature, and texture of blade.

The important thing about a sword, however, is how effective it is as a weapon. Is the katana, in fact, superior to other swords made elsewhere? Most experts agree that it is. Sir George Sansom, one of the greatest present day authorities on Japan, says that for strength and edge the Japanese sword of the thirteenth century excels all others made in any other country before or since. And in his six-volume study of Japan's history, arts, and literature, Captain Frank Brinkley calls the katana unequalled. He says that if the Japanese had never produced anything but this sword, we would still have to respect them profoundly for their craftsmanship and their scientific understanding of cause and effect.

There are many ways in which the excellence of the Japanese sword can be demonstrated. Two of the famous swords named in the *Heike Monogatari* were Beard-cutter and Knee-cutter. They got these names because, as was customary in earlier and more barbaric times, after they were forged they were tested by being used to execute two criminals. Each of these swords not only cut off the head of a condemned man at one stroke, but *Hige-kiri* also cut off the beard of one of them, and *Hiza-kiri* cut off the others knees.

But, after all, a razor is sharp, too. What about durability? One of the strongest tests of this was made near the end of the nineteenth century by George Hutterott, a German who was visiting Japan. He piled five coins on top of one another and then cut through them—a full half-inch of bronze—at one blow, and without injuring the edge of the blade.

A final important factor in a sword is its balance, and here again the samurai sword is demonstrably superior to any that were made in the west. The katana is not heavy—it generally weighs between two and three pounds—and, since it was made to be used with either one or two hands, it has a long hilt which acts as a counter-balance to the blade. It was once a form of punishment in the British cavalry to make a trooper stand at attention with his badly balanced sabre fully extended. In a few minutes his arm would begin to ache agonizingly from the strain. But a katana with a blade of equal length, and infinitely better cutting edge, can be held in this same position for a much longer time with no difficulty at all.

While a few famous swords in the west—Nothung, Excalibur and Durandel—were supposed to have special or magical qualities, almost all well-known Japanese swords were believed to have them. After having first been called Beard-cutter, the name of the famous Minamoto sword was changed several times. When it came into the hands of Yoshitomo, father of Yoshitsune, it was called Companion-cutter because of something that had happened years before. It had stood one night against a wall next to Little Crow. During the night both swords fell down with a clatter and, when they were examined, it was found that though Little Crow had originally been slightly longer, they were now both the same length. It was believed that Beard-cutter had magically cut its companion sword down to its size.

During his first campaigns against the Taira, Yoshitomo was badly defeated and felt that the sword had lost its effectiveness. Hachiman, the war god, supposedly came to him in a dream and told him this was because the name of the sword had been changed. Yoshitomo immediately changed its name back to Beard-cutter, and in his next battle he found that the sword was itself again. He won a great victory.

Noble families treasured an ancestral blade not only as a weapon but as a symbol and a talisman. If, by some misfortune, it passed from their hands, they felt that their luck had gone with it. The samurai took such pride in their right to wear their swords that when Uesugi Kenshin, one of the feudal chiefs of the sixteenth century, enacted a code of regulations for his fighting men, the severest penalty he could devise was to deprive a samurai of that right. It is recorded that when one of his vassals, Nagao Uemon, was condemned to forfeit the privilege of wearing a sword because of a serious offense, he reminded his lord of the great deeds his father had done on Kenshin's behalf. Kenshin agreed to commute his sentence and let him kill himself instead.

As might be expected of a ceremonious people, the Japanese had rigid rules on the wearing and handling of swords. Ancient etiquette required that you bow to a sword before examining it. Then, sitting and holding the sheath in the left hand with the edge upward, you drew the sword slowly and gracefully. In the story of Yoshitsune it is told that when the horse of a high Taira official spattered the scabbard of

Yoshitsune's sword with mud, Yoshitsune promptly pulled him from the saddle and cut off his head.

For a samurai to clash the scabbard of his sword against that of another samurai was a serious breach of etiquette. To step over a sword that was lying on the ground was an insult. But to lay one's own sword on the ground and kick the hilt towards another man was the greatest insult of all, a challenge to fight to the death.

"Foreign swords are forged with the most practical and materialistic end in view," said Sojiro Suto, an expert on the Japanese sword. "If a sword be keen enough to cut or pierce things, it is considered enough. But in Japan the sword stands for the defense of the individual and the nation."

In his authoritative *Handbook on the Samurai Sword,* John Yumoto says, "In ancient times it was well established that anything suitable as an offering to the gods had to possess three elements: purity, rarity and value." The Japanese sword has all of these elements and more; and because it represents so much that is truly Japanese, it is not surprising that it should be one of the Three Treasures.

9

The Jewel

THE THIRD of the Three Treasures which were given
to Ninigi by Amaterasu was the Jewel. Jewels of great
price have always been part of the regalia, the official
and ceremonial ornaments, of royalty. In this case,
however, the Jewel was not a diamond, emerald, ruby,
or other precious stone but, at the most, a semi-precious one: agate, jasper, jade, or chrysoprase. In
other words, its value lay not in the price or rarity of
the stone itself, but in its history, associations and,
possibly most important, in its symbolism. And
whether this particular curved jewel, like the other
magatama found in the early burial mounds, is an
amulet that represents the claw or tusk of a tiger or
bear or whether—as some scholars think—it stands
for the moon (with the Mirror representing the sun
and the Sword the lightning flash), it still remains a

natural object. It represents some kind of natural phenomenon and, intentionally or not, this underlines one of the most basic elements in the Japanese character: their love of nature.

The earliest form of Shinto was based on an appreciation of nature, rather than a fear of it. Proof of this attitude toward nature can be found almost anywhere in Japan today. The *torii* is the sacred arch or gateway that serves as an entrance to a temple or shrine. While it is generally made of wood, it can also be made of stone or even metal. But its form is always the same: two columns leaning slightly in to the center, a top crossbar with projecting ends, and another crossbar under it. There is some question about how its shape and name originated. Most authorities believe, however, that it is a larger version of the perches on which the sacred cocks rested when they greeted

Amaterasu, the Sun Goddess, every morning; and
they believe that the word *torii* derives from *tori,* a
bird, and *iru,* to perch.

Whatever its origin, torii are one of the most
common sights in Japan. They are seen most frequently of course when approaching a temple or shrine.
But they are often found in unexpected places: at the
beginning of a mountain path, deep in the woods, or
on the edge of a lake. If one goes through such a torii,
one may find a spring or a tree or rock of unusual
shape or size; some natural object with special qualities that made it seem worthy of worship. But often
when the traveller passes through one, he will find
none of these things on the far side, but only a view
that is so beautiful or impressive that it, too, is considered sacred, as sacred as a temple or a shrine.

While this love of nature is understandable
among poets and artists, among courtiers with the
leisure to enjoy it, and even among the peasants who
are dependent on the earth for their livelihood, it is
somewhat surprising to find it also among warriors.
But it was just as strong among the samurai as it was
among other groups in Japanese society, possibly because certain changing aspects of nature suggested
that life was all the more beautiful because it was
transient. In any case, a love and appreciation of nature played an important part in the life of even the
sternest warrior.

"The summer grasses: all that remain of the warrior's dream!" wrote the poet Basho on visiting the
site of a famous battlefield. And when Prince Otsu
was about to be executed in the year 687, he wrote
this poem:

Today, looking for the last time at the mallards
Who call to each other on the pond of Iware,
Must I vanish into the clouds.

One of the first castles in Japan that can be compared to those built in Europe during the Middle Ages—that is, of a purely defensive type—was the one that was built at Osaka by Hideyoshi. And despite the fact that it was so strong that it could only be taken by a strategem, it was a thing of beauty as well as a stronghold. The keeps of Japanese castles are beautifully proportioned, each story being slightly smaller than the one below it, with curving roof lines that are crowned with gold or copper carp or dragons.

When Ieyasu built his castle at Yedo—a far larger one than Hideyoshi's—he had the ramparts covered with earth and pines planted and trained to stretch their limbs over the wide moats. In this mixture of the beautiful and the functional, the love of nature combined with the work of man, we find the essence of the Japanese character.

The most important early influence on Japanese art was, of course, China. With Chinese civilization at a much higher level than their own, particularly during the Nara period, it was inevitable that Japanese artists should imitate the work of Chinese artists. For many years the Japanese artist was more interested in copying the work of Chinese masters than in looking at his own world and attempting to portray it in a style of his own. But by the end of the tenth century Japanese painting began to develop in a manner that had almost nothing left of the Chinese in it. The long, horizontal scrolls that were produced at this time were filled with life and showed scenes of battles and journeys, while the Chinese paintings of this and later periods concentrated on landscapes of a very specific mood. The chief difference between the two schools was that the Chinese were principally interested in philosophy, and this was reflected in the landscapes they painted; the Japanese, on the other hand, had suddenly discovered man and were beginning to show him in the real world in which he lived. This particular type of art reached its peak in the thirteenth century with the Kamakura warrior scrolls that are full of battles and burnings, fleeing peasants, and fighting samurai.

Though Zen Buddhism came to Japan at an earlier date, it was during the Kamakura period that it began to exert its full influence on Japanese art. One of the goals of Zen was to achieve a state in which one was no longer aware of the self. Although meditation was important in reaching this goal, it could not be reached by meditation alone, but only in conjunction with some meaningful activity. Thus the Zen artist worked at developing his skill, learning every possible brush stroke or combination of strokes, until he no longer had to think of technique. It was then possible for him to reach a state in which the feeling was, "It is not I who am doing this. It is just happening."

It was this process—the learning of technique until it required no conscious thought—that enabled the Zen artist to work so quickly, making every brush stroke count and simplifying the whole so that what he painted was the essence of what he was trying to show. Some of the finest examples of this particular kind of work were done by Sesshu, who lived during the fifteenth century.

When the Japanese—and particularly the samu-

rai—adopted Zen Buddhism, it had an effect on the
construction of their houses as well as other things.
Until that time there had been very little privacy in
Japanese houses. But now the practitioner of Zen
fitted up a room for meditation called a *sho-in* or study.
Instead of bamboo blinds and latticed shutters, sliding
screens covered with translucent rice paper were installed. These *shoji* screens had originally been used
in the monasteries and the houses of Zen monks. They
made a pleasant room since they let in light, but could
not be seen through. Also borrowed from the Zen
monasteries was an alcove in which a sacred picture
could be hung or an image of Buddha placed to serve
as an object of contemplation.

The advent of Zen affected the surroundings of
a house as well as its interior. During the Heian period, the nobility had become very interested in the
designing and creating of parks with miniature lakes,
islands, and rock gardens. Sometimes attempts were
made to reproduce natural landscapes, but generally
speaking the gardens were Chinese in character, formal and conventional. It was not until the time of the
Kamakura administration that, with the help of Zen
teachings, a new approach to gardening developed.

Originally the plan for a park or garden was
worked out by an artist. But since Buddhist temples
had always been built with the most careful considera-
tion of their surroundings, Buddhist monks gradually
came to be recognized as the masters of this art. At
the beginning of the thirteenth century, Gokyogoku
wrote a treatise on gardening which was based on
Buddhist principles. In part, it said that in nature
everything comes in pairs: the male and the female,
the dominant and the dominated. By defining every-

thing that went into a garden, he gave everything a meaning and thus laid down rules on how the elements should be arranged and combined. A lake had to be shaped like a tortoise or a crane, symbols of long life. An island might be a mountain, the bank of a stream, a strip of seashore, or a cloud in the distance.

These principles were later elaborated on by a monk named Soseki. And in the second half of the fifteenth century, the system was further extended by the artist priest Soami. Soami listed twelve different varieties of landscapes and waterscapes and indicated what should go into each. Thus, in rock gardens, he placed: sea and river stones; stones from mountains and from the plains; current stones and wave stones: stones from which a stream flows; stones that divide a stream; and stones against which a stream breaks. He also had categories for islands and shores as well as rocks, trees, and flowers, each with its own name and meaning.

Although the earlier parks and gardens were very large, by following the principles laid down by the masters of landscape gardening, it was possible for the samurai and the man of limited means to create gardens which, while small, were among the most beautiful in the world. Rocks played an important part in these gardens. They were selected with as much care as the Western gardener expends in selecting a special type of flower or shrub. Huge rocks were transported for great distances, and wealthy men paid enormous sums for ones with certain special shapes, coloring, or texture. Today, the Japanese gardener recognizes one hundred and thirty-eight types of stones and rocks having special names and functions, in addition to others of secondary importance.

Besides flower beds, one of the chief characteristics of the Western garden is its lawn. But a lawn, to
the Japanese, seems artificial, since it is almost never
found in nature. So, in many cases, the rock and tree
groupings in a garden are surrounded by sand or pebbles of carefully selected size and color. These sand or
pebble areas are carefully raked in a variety of patterns that have different names and meanings. The
areas of sand or pebbles, with the rake marks that give
it texture, flowing around a rock or tree are every bit
as beautiful as an expanse of lawn that gets its texture
from the play of light and shade.

In our gardens the accent is on the form—on
what is actually there—but in Japanese gardens the
accent is on the spirit, that which is suggested being
more important than that which is actually seen. Thus,
when the great Zen tea-master, Sen no Rikyu, built a
garden at Sakai, he planted a row of evergreens to hide
the view of the sea. When guests entered the garden,
they walked over stepping stones to reach the stone
water basin where they washed their hands and rinsed
their mouths. It was only when they were in this humble position, when they bent over to scoop up the
water, that they could catch a glimpse of the sea in the
distance. But at that moment the visitor had a sense of
the Oneness of all things, felt the relationship between
himself, the water in the dipper, and the ocean.

If it seems strange to us to think of a samurai,
with his swords in his sash, working in his garden or
pruning one of the dwarf trees that were grown in pots
and called *bonsai,* it may seem even stranger to find
him involved in the elaborate ritual of the tea ceremony. Yet this was an interest that amounted to a
passion with many of the most famous fighting men of

Japan; and, since it, too, was rooted in Zen, it had many things in common with gardening.

Tea was first introduced into Japan from China early in the ninth century. It was originally drunk by Zen priests to help them keep awake through long periods of meditation. For a time, during the early days of the Kamakura administration, it was considered a kind of medicine, particularly a cure for drunkenness. But around the middle of the thirteenth century the ceremony of tea drinking began to develop, based on the custom of serving tea to visitors at the Zen monasteries. By the time of the Ashikaga Shoguns, it had left the monasteries and become an elaborate ritual practised by both the nobility and the samurai.

Specialists in the art of serving tea called tea-masters arose, and special places in which to drink it were built. Sometimes these were elaborate pavilions, but generally they were small rustic huts looking out on to gardens. Every detail of the ceremony, from the size and furnishing of the room to the behavior of the host and guests was specified.

The appeal of the tea ceremony for the wealthy aristocrat and its appeal for the fighting man were related, but opposite. It brought to the court noble, for a time at least, some of the virtues which the samurai practiced in the simplicity of his life. To the samurai, it offered refinement without making him feel self-indulgent or effeminate. For the tea cult combined culture with simplicity. As the participant in the tea ceremony sat in the tiny room, handling utensils of a rude type and looking out on a garden, he felt himself to be a kind of monk, giving up all forms of luxury; but at the same time he was cultivating artistic tastes that separated him from the common people.

There were many different types of *cha-no-yu* or tea ceremonies, depending on the time of day and what was served in addition to tea. But the basic procedure in all of them was the same. The guests, usually no more than four or five, entered the garden through a special gate and waited in a special area. Generally there was a bench for them to sit on, placed so that it gave them the best view of the garden.

When the host received word that the guests had arrived, he immediately went to the tea pavilion and continued preparations that he had begun earlier. The tea pavilion was small, low-ceilinged, and completely bare. The wood floor was covered with *tatami* or straw mats. In one corner of the room was a *tokonoma* or alcove, and in this was hung a scroll that could be either a painting or a specimen of calligraphy. This

was called a *kakemono* and, with possibly a flower arrangement, was the only decoration in the room.

In the floor was a small opening that was used as a fireplace. On this water was heating in a handsome iron kettle. The host now mended the fire, cleared away the ashes, and swept the mats with a small hand brush. Then he went to the door of the teahouse, greeted his guests, and returned to his place near the fire, leaving the door of the pavilion partly open.

The guests would now wash their hands in order of their rank, either at a stone basin in the garden or at a ewer placed near the door. After washing, they would enter the pavilion one by one, go to the alcove and examine the scroll hanging there, then go to the fireplace and inspect the teakettle. The place where each was to sit was specified and so was the order of conversation. The first subject was the scroll in the alcove. When the guests had each expressed their opinion of it, the host prepared the tea.

Powdered tea was taken from a jar, placed in a drinking cup, and water from the kettle was poured over it. Then the cup was passed to the first guest with a neatly folded napkin. He sipped the tea, wiped the cup with the napkin, and passed it back to the host. The host then gave it to the second guest and so on, the last guest being careful to finish it. Then the cup went around again by itself to be examined.

Even in this comparatively simple version of the tea ceremony, there were many points of etiquette to be observed. Every article used in the ceremony, even the charcoal and the container in which it was kept, was examined separately by the guests at certain specified times and in a specified order. The whole tea ceremony was, in fact, an elaborate ritual which both host and guests had to learn through long instruction.

While the utensils were supposed to be extremely plain—the tea scoop carved from a piece of bamboo, for instance—there was sometimes great ostentation hidden in the simplicity. Rich noblemen would sometimes pay fortunes for supposedly simple articles that had acquired value through their association with famous tea-masters or other personages. There is a Korean peasant's rice bowl, for instance, called the *Ido* which was brought from Korea in the early seventeenth century. It came into the hands of a celebrated tea-master, was used more than once by a Shogun, and when it was sold, during the 1930's, it was for a price that was close to a hundred thousand dollars.

Yet all this elaborate ritual and hidden show of wealth runs counter to the true meaning of the tea ceremony. Nakano Kazuma, a famous tea-master, once said: "The spirit of cha-no-yu is to cleanse the senses from contamination. By seeing the kakemono in the tokonoma and smelling the flower in the vase, one's sight and sense of smell is cleansed; by listening to the boiling of water in the iron kettle and the dripping of water from the bamboo pipe, one's ears are cleansed; by tasting tea, one's mouth is cleansed; and by handling the tea utensils, one's sense of touch is cleansed. When all the sense organs are thus cleansed, the mind itself is cleansed of defilements. The art of tea is after all a spiritual discipline, and my aspiration for every hour of the day is not to depart from the spirit of the tea, which is by no means a matter of mere entertainment."

Despite its complicated procedure and trappings, the true spirit of the tea ceremony is actually something very simple. It was and is a gathering of four or five old friends in a small room with little else in it but what is needed to prepare and drink tea.

Since they are old friends and all students of Zen, their attitude towards most things would be similar, the talk would be easy and relaxed, and they would naturally be interested in their host's possessions: his favorite painting and tea caddy. They would talk about these things and anything else that seemed related—philosophy, ethics or history—and come away from the gathering both stimulated and refreshed.

When the simplicity of the tea ceremony or anything related to it was affected and not real, when there was a false note of any sort, a tea-master could sense it immediately. It is said that Sen no Rikyu went with his son to call on a fellow practitioner of the art and that his son admired the old, moss-covered gate that led into the garden. But Sen no Rikyu did not.

"It is not from these parts," he said. "It looks as if it had been brought here from some ancient mountain temple at considerable expense. A simple wicket made by a local farmer would have done just as well, given the place a rustic and unpretentious look, and would not have made us think of difficulty and expense. I doubt if we shall have a very interesting tea ceremony here."

Thus, though the samurai was one of the fiercest fighting men in the world—a warrior whose training was more rigorous and habits more spartan than the knights of Europe—his life had another side to it. For Zen Buddhism and his love of nature, reflected in his interest in art, gardening, and the tea ceremony, gave it balance. It was this balance that made him quite different from almost any other professional military man who has ever existed.

10

The Making of a Samurai

THE Age of Chivalry in Europe is generally considered to have begun in the latter part of the eleventh century, shortly after the Norman Conquest, and to have ended in the early part of the sixteenth century.

The Age of the Samurai can be said to have begun in the latter part of the twelfth century with the establishment of the Kamakura administration, but it continued to exist until fairly late in the nineteenth century—until, in fact, several years after the end of the American Civil War.

The story of chivalry is a familiar one to us and so is the way in which one became a knight. The candidate was generally a member of the feudal nobility. He began his training as a page, learning knightly behavior and service at the castle of a lord or the manor of a knight. When he was about eighteen, he became a squire; and when he was sufficiently skilled or had distinguished himself in battle, he was either initiated into knighthood with formal ceremonies or knighted on the field of battle. All during this time, in addition to knightly pursuits such as falconry and hunting, he was learning horsemanship and being trained in the use of weapons, particularly the lance and the sword.

While the way in which one became a samurai was similar to this in some respects, in others it was quite different. Originally a samurai was a royal guard, a member of one of the old clans who were the hereditary escorts of the sovereign. But they were by no means the only warriors in Japan nor was the term applied to a whole class of warriors. Not until the twelfth century, when the Minamoto family took over the rule of Japan, was the feudal tradition finally and firmly fixed. It was then that the samurai became a distinct caste with higher and lower grades. At this time they were mounted, wore heavier armor than the foot soldiers, and bore a heraldic insignia. They were thus very much like the knights in western Europe, owing allegiance to a lord and being given regular allowances in rice and property in exchange for their services. And like the European knights, a warrior— no matter how brave and skillful—could not become a samurai automatically. Unless he was born in that class, he could only become a samurai by special permission of the Shogun.

Once a European became a knight, however, he remained one until the day he died. In Japan, this was not always so. When a samurai's feudal lord lost his estates so that he could not support his followers, or died without leaving an heir to whom the warrior could give his allegiance, the samurai became a *ronin*, a warrior without a master or attachments. He might continue as a ronin, sacrificing many of the privileges of a samurai, but he usually sought service with another lord, becoming his retainer.

When the son of a samurai was five years old, he was placed on a *go* board, which is similar to a chessboard, a sash was tied around his waist, and he was given a small sword so that he could become accustomed to carrying it. At about the age of fifteen the ceremony of *gembuku* was performed, rites that symbolized the fact that he had become a man. The front part of his head was shaved, his name was changed as a sign that he had left his childhood behind him, and he was given the real swords that he would carry for the rest of his life. At this same time, he was taken before his family's feudal lord and asked to be permitted to enter his service.

Long before this, however, he would have begun his training. Depending on the times—on whether or not his lord was actively engaged in warfare—he might or might not have begun learning to read and write. But his parents would certainly have begun preparing him for the physical rigors of a samurai's life. Almost from the time he was able to walk, he would have been taught to endure pain, cold, and hunger. He would have risen often before dawn to bathe in icy streams and would have travelled long distances barefoot in winter.

At the same time, he would have begun to learn to use weapons. In earliest times, and until about the ninth or tenth century, the bow was the Japanese warrior's favorite weapon. It is difficult to make comparisons, but probably the best of the ancient Japanese archers were at least the equal of the English bowmen during the great period of English archery when they broke the power of the French knights at Crecy, Poitiers, and Agincourt.

The Japanese bow differed considerably from the English longbow, and the shooting techniques differed also. The English longbow was generally about six feet long, a straight "self" bow, made out of one piece of wood, usually yew. The most ancient Japanese bow was also a "self" bow, usually made of boxwood. But many years before the days of the Samurai, it had become a compound bow, made of strips of wood—in most cases bamboo—glued together and bound with cord or rattan for strength. And, instead of being straight, it was recurved. That is, when unstrung, the top and bottom limbs curved away from the archer. When strung, the limbs were pulled into a taut double curve like a Cupid's bow. This recurving increased the speed and power with which the arrow was hurled from the string. In addition, it was longer than the English longbow; the Japanese bow was from seven to nine feet long, and it was not symmetrical: the upper limb or portion above the hand grip was twice as long as the lower limb.

All these elements combined to give the Japanese bow tremendous power. When the first iron shield was brought to Japan from Korea in the fourth century, the Emperor Nintoku asked one of his archers to test it, and the bowman easily pierced it with an arrow. This was something that the English war bow could do also some nine centuries later; but, because of its length, the English longbow could not be used on horseback, while the even longer Japanese bow with its short lower limb could be.

The Japanese shooting technique differed from

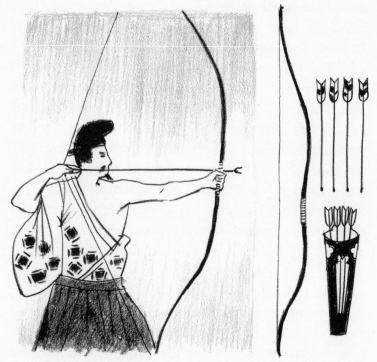

the Western method as much as the bows differed. In the West, the arrow is placed on the left side of the bow, the bow is held level with the left arm extended and the bowstrings grasped by the three middle fingers of the right hand, with the arrow nock between the top two fingers. The right arm does the drawing. The old English archers generally drew to the ear; contemporary archers draw to the cheekbone or the corner of the mouth.

The Japanese laid their arrow on the right side of the bow, hooked the string with their thumb and, raising the bow above their heads, drew it with both hands simultaneously as they lowered it; drawing, not to the cheek or the ear, but to a point well behind the head. This draw enabled them to use arrows from three-and-a-half to four feet long.

In addition to accuracy and power, the important thing about a war bow is the speed with which it can be used. We have concrete evidence of the power of the Japanese bow and the speed, strength, and endurance of the Japanese archers. In Kyoto there is a temple with a veranda one hundred and twenty-eight yards long and sixteen feet high. It is obvious that with such limited elevation, it would take a bow of considerable power to carry the length of the veranda. But in 1686 Wada Daihachi sent eight thousand, one hundred and thirty-three arrows the length of the corridor from sunset to sunset, an average of about five shafts a minute during twenty-four consecutive hours. Though this sounds incredible, it was nearly equalled in 1852 by Tsuruta Masatoki in a temple with similar dimensions in Tokyo. He fired ten thousand and fifty shafts in twenty hours, an average of nine shafts a minute, and more than half of them carried the full length of the veranda. American bows and archers are generally considered to be the best in the world today. But there is no Western archer living who could come even close to duplicating this feat, and it is very doubtful that one of the old English archers could have done so.

Though the bow was the favorite weapon of the Japanese warrior for many centuries, once the katana was developed it soon took the place of the bow in his affection. Swordsmanship became as important a skill as archery had been in the past.

Even if one is not a swordsman, one has only to look at a katana to realize that Japanese swordsmanship would be quite different from any Western type. With its long hilt and curved, keen edge, it is obvious that it would be almost impossible to parry a full, two-

handed cut from a Japanese sword. A swordsman had
to rely on his speed and agility to avoid any stroke that
was made at him, rather than attempting to ward it off
with his own sword. This explains the descriptions of
the famous battle between Yoshitsune and Benkei on
the Gojo bridge when Yoshitsune never even drew his
sword, but was content to avoid the mighty strokes of
Benkei's naginata. Agility was a very important part of
combat, and therefore valued as highly as the ability to
wield a sword.

Because of its excellent balance, the Japanese
sword can be used either one or two-handed, but it is
usually held with both hands. The right hand is placed
close to the guard and the left back a few inches. The
point is held up, and the hilt about three-quarters of
an arm's-length from the body. The point is almost
never used and the cuts are almost entirely downward
or horizontal.

There are some sixteen varieties of cuts in Japanese swordplay. Each has its own name, such as the
wheelstroke, the cleaver, the torso-severer, the pear-
splitter, the thunder stroke, and the scarf sweep. Each
of these, although it sounds poetic and fanciful, carries an exact meaning to a Japanese swordsman.

Once Zen was adopted by the warrior class, it
also began to play an important part in swordsmanship. The thought of death was a great problem for
the samurai since his life was devoted to fighting, and
fighting is bound to mean death for someone. Zen
helped the samurai reach a state of mind where he
could face death with calm resolution, but it did more
than that for him. Zen was not something that could
exist by itself in a vacuum, but only along with and
through some other activity. For the swordsman this

meant constant practice in the use of his weapon, practice that might go on for years until every possible move in swordplay had become second nature to him and completely instinctive. It was only then that he could achieve *muga,* the complete unconsciousness of self in which the feeling was, "It is not I who am doing this." In other words, the swordsman and the sword were one. He did not have to think of what he was going to do and how he was going to do it. He merely did it.

A story is told of a young man who came to an elderly, retired master swordsman who lived in a lonely mountain hut. The young man asked for instruction. The old swordsman agreed and put him to work cutting wood and drawing water, cleaning the hut, and cooking for him. When this had gone on for some time and the old swordsman had not even mentioned swordsmanship to him, much less begun to instruct him in the art, the young man protested, explaining that he had not come there to act as a servant. The master looked at him, but did not say anything. A short while later, however, while the young man was preparing their evening rice, the old swordsman stole up behind him and struck him with a stick. Again the young man protested, and again the old swordsman said nothing.

After that, the young man could not relax for a moment. No matter what he was doing—chopping wood, working in the garden, or cleaning the house— his master would appear beside him or behind him and strike him. To the young man's credit, he remained with the old swordsman and, after more than a year of this harassment had gone by, he became so agile that he could dodge any blow no matter how unexpected.

One day, when the old swordsman was preparing tea, the young man crept up behind him with a stick in his hand and struck a sudden blow at the back of the old man's head. But it never reached its mark, for the old man caught it with the cover of the kettle. In that moment the young man's eyes were opened and he suddenly realized what his master had been trying to teach him. He also realized that only now was he ready to begin learning to use a sword.

The study of Zen, along with the study of swordsmanship, prepared a samurai to face any opponent. But when he was facing him, he had to maintain his *muga,* his detached and free-flowing state of awareness. If he did not, the Zen master swordsmen believed, if he began to think of either danger or the need for technique, a *suki* would appear: a chink or crack in his attention, a momentary relaxation of tension that could be fatal. This was what he guarded against in himself and what he watched for in his opponent. For this was the moment to strike.

There is an interesting illustration of this, and of Japanese swordsmanship in general, in the Japanese film, *The Magnificent Seven.* For though swordplay on the stage and screen in the West is rehearsed and exaggerated for dramatic effect, it is still based on authentic fencing principles and the actors involved study under a fencing master. The same is true of Japanese films, and in them one can see at least an approximation of swordplay in the days of the samurai. In the movie, a somewhat arrogant samurai has challenged another to a test of skill. They first face each other with bamboo staves which they hold and wield like swords. They continue to face each other, staves raised in the guard position, for several moments, unmoving. Then, as the arrogant samurai strikes, the quiet samurai strikes also, but a shade more quickly.

"Got you!" says the first samurai.

His quiet opponent shakes his head. "If these had been real swords," he says, "you would be dead."

Infuriated, the arrogant samurai insists that they try it again, this time with their swords. Reluctantly the quiet samurai draws his katana, and again they face each other. Again there are several long moments of quiet tension in which neither moves; then, as the arrogant samurai strikes, his quiet opponent strikes also—so quickly that his blade is a blur—and, as he had said, his opponent falls dead.

In Western fencing, no matter how violent the beginning of an engagement may seem, the initial moments are really spent in feeling out an opponent, testing his strength, speed and skill, and searching for his weaknesses. And in a different way, this was precisely what was happening between the two samurai before a blow was struck. They were feeling each other out mentally, searching for a suki, and when one thought he had found one, he made his move. This was the only way in which combat could be conducted, for the katana was such a deadly weapon that only seldom were more than two or three passes exchanged. Therefore the testing, the feeling out process, had to take place *before* the engagement began.

This process had its parallel in our old West—when two gunmen faced each other, each waiting for the other to make his play. There was even further similarity between this and Japanese swordplay. For one of the things that the Western gunman prided himself on was the speed of his draw. And this was something a samurai practiced as tirelessly as a gun slinger —and for exactly the same reason: because his life might depend on it.

For a samurai to draw his sword in many places, particularly in the castle of a feudal lord, was punishable by death. However if his opponent drew first, drawing his sword was considered self-defense. Therefore it was not uncommon for a warrior to goad another into drawing and then try and beat him to the first stroke. Since the katana was worn in the sash with the cutting edge up, it was possible to combine the draw with a lightning slash in what was called *I-ai*. A full I-ai involved a draw, a slash and a return of the sword to the scabbard. A skilled swordsman could perform this feat with almost incredible speed, as can be seen in I-ai contests still held in Japan where contestants not only demonstrate their speed, but their ability to cut through a bamboo pole six inches thick.

Along with archery and swordsmanship, the young samurai learned to use other weapons such as the spear and halberd or naginata and, after the latter part of the sixteenth century, the match-lock or arquebus. But besides learning how to use weapons, the samurai learned how to fight and defend himself without them, either with his bare hands or with any object within reach. This ancient art was known as *shinobi, yawara* or *ju-jutsu*. These made use of an adversary's own strength to bring about his downfall, and it is upon them that present day *judo* and *karate* are based. There are many cases on record of samurai, unable to use their swords, who killed armed adversaries with pieces of firewood or brazier irons or who defended themselves with umbrellas or pot covers.

Having learned how to fight with and without

weapons, horsemanship, the principles of Zen, and military tactics and history, the samurai was a magnificent fighting man. He was probably one of the best-trained warriors the world has ever known. In times of war he went into battle in the service of his feudal lord, sometimes at the age of sixteen or seventeen. At other times, samurai who wanted to perfect themselves in all their skills would travel all over Japan, undergoing all sorts of hardships and studying at different schools of swordsmanship. In this they were following the example of the Zen monks who also travelled throughout Japan, studying under different teachers, before they attained final enlightenment. Among the samurai this was known as *musha-shugyo* or training in warriorship.

While there were undoubtedly some bullies and braggarts among the samurai—as there always have been among military men—the best of them, especially the ones who had truly understood Zen teachings, were modest and unassuming. They were so conscious of their warlike skills, that they had no need to make a show of them. Tsukahara Bokuden, one of the greatest swordsmen of the sixteenth century, illustrated this one day when he was crossing Lake Biwa in a boat with many other passengers. Among them was another samurai who boasted loudly of his skill in swordsmanship. Bokuden sat near the stern, half-dozing and saying nothing. This irritated the other samurai so much that he finally approached him, shook him, and said, "You also carry two swords. Why have you not said anything?"

"Because my art is quite different from yours," said Bokuden. "It is not concerned with defeating others, but in not being defeated."

"Is that so? What school do you belong to, then?"

"It is known as the *mutekatsu* school." (Meaning to defeat an enemy without hands; that is, without using a sword.)

"Why do you carry a sword then?"

"As a constant reminder that I must do away with all selfish motives and not injure others."

This further infuriated the other samurai. "You mean you could fight me without a sword?" he demanded.

"Of course," said Bokuden.

The angry samurai immediately ordered the boatman to row them to shore, but Bokuden suggested that they go to a nearby island instead where they would not be disturbed and would not disturb others with their combat. The samurai agreed and, when they reached the island, he jumped ashore and drew his sword, waiting for Bokuden. Bokuden took his own swords from his sash and handed them to the boatman. Then, instead of going ashore also, he picked up one of the oars and pushed the boat out into deep water.

"This," said Bokuden to the marooned samurai, "is my 'no-sword' school."

From the earliest times the Japanese warrior wore armor, and he continued to wear some pieces of it until late in the nineteenth century. The history of Japanese armor is as extensive as the history of the sword. Before the eighth century, armor was called *kawara*. It was generally made of fairly large plates of metal fastened together and made to go around the body and meet in the front like a kimono. This armor was apparently quite satisfactory when fighting on foot, but when horses were introduced from the continent and warriors began fighting on horseback, something lighter and more flexible was needed. So a different type of armor came into use, made of either smaller plates of metal or layers of leather. These were overlapped like scales and fastened together with leather thongs or braid.

During the Heian period, fighting on horseback became the usual method of combat. Since the warrior used a bow and arrow as well as a sword while mounted, he needed to have both hands free and could not carry a shield. Therefore, at about this time, shoulder protectors called *sode* were developed. These were flaps which were attached to the body armor by four cords in such a way that they moved backward and forward with the arm, protecting the upper arm and the side beneath it.

One of the major differences between European and Japanese armor is that while European armor generally took its shape from the costume of the period, Japanese armor never bore any resemblance to ordinary garments. The knight of the Middle Ages, encased in steel armor, seemed to be wearing a suit of metal clothes. The Japanese warrior, on the other hand, looked as if he were wearing protective curtains. Japanese armor was, in fact, suspended from the body rather than fitted to it.

Japanese armor was both decorated and highly decorative. The metal or leather scales were fastened together with brightly colored cords. Various parts of the armor were plated or inlaid with gold or silver or painted with lacquer. Though helmets were originally simple, they later became quite ornate. During the Kamakura period they began to be made with *kuwagata* or antlers projecting from them. Sometimes a piece of silk called a *horo* was stretched between the horns of the helmet or thrown over them and allowed to hang down in front and in back. While it may have appeared decorative also, the chief purpose of the horo was to deflect arrows.

The introduction of firearms had some effect on warfare in Japan, but it did not have the great effect that it had in Europe. Though artillery was used and castles became more massive and, at least in their protective features, more like the castles in the West, battles continued to be fought in much the same way as they had always been. Strategy as we know it today, even the tactical plan for an individual battle, did not come into general use before the first half of the sixteenth century. Before that, though some use was made of tactical formations, a battle resembled a giant fencing match with every man fighting as an individual so that the engagement consisted of a series of personal duels all in progress together.

It was the custom of a samurai to proclaim his name and title to a single enemy, adding any details from his own exploits or those of his ancestors that would glorify his name and intimidate his opponents. The enemy would do the same, and the warriors would then engage one another. They were generally permitted to finish their combat undisturbed, though the victor was frequently attacked by the comrades or retainers of the man who was vanquished.

It has been said that the samurai was one of the bravest and best trained fighting men in the world. Possibly it was because of this, and because of his extreme individualism, that Japan did not develop any great military strategists until very late in her history.

II

Bushido

or the Knightly Code

JUST AS the training of the samurai was like that of the medieval knight in some ways and different in others, so were there both similarities and differences in the rules that governed their conduct and the customs they observed.

When we talk of chivalry we mean the customs and ideals, as well as the duties and privileges, of European knights during the Middle Ages. Most of these customs stemmed from the requirements of the feudal system, the loyalty owed by a knight to his lord. But they were also strongly influenced by the Church, which adopted and modified them for its own ends, and by the medieval attitude towards women which was based on reverence for the Virgin Mary.

In *Le Morte d'Arthur,* the King Arthur story, damsels in distress were constantly appealing to knights for aid. The influence of the Church can be seen in this statement by a hermit to Sir Gawaine: "When ye were first made knight, ye should have taken ye to knightly deeds and virtuous living, but ye have not done so, for ye have lived mischievously many winters. But Sir Galahad is pure and has sinned never, and that is the cause he shall achieve where he goeth that ye nor none shall not attain."

The samurai's code was also an outgrowth of a feudal system. Its keynote was loyalty, too. But it was never tempered by the European knight's devotion to either women or religious principles, except as a personal thing. Though the Japanese feudal warrior might pray to the god of war and be a devout Buddhist, he did not fight religious crusades like the knights of the West. He did not go into battle following a sacred banner and calling on the names of angels and saints. He proclaimed his own name and lineage. And while there had been important empresses in Japan's past, and the feminine influence was strong in the imperial court, the feudal warrior of Japan did not ride forth to rescue damsels in distress. He would have found it both shocking and incredible that a fighting man should risk his life, a life that belonged to his feudal lord, in combat for a lady's favor.

The differences between the two codes had their roots in the differences between the two cultures and also in geographical differences. During the Middle Ages, Western knights were in constant conflict with heathen warriors. When they fought for the Christian church, they were also fighting for Christian territory. In Japan there was no connection between feudal and religious interests. Even during the time of the Mongol invasions it would have been useless to try and rouse the warriors of the island kingdom by crying that the Faith was in danger; for the Mongols were as much Buddhists as the Japanese.

While feudalism and the age of chivalry lasted about four hundred years in Europe, it lasted until the latter part of the nineteenth century in Japan. This was at least partly because of her self-imposed isolation from the rest of the world. There were no influences great enough to change a culture where traditions were so strong and all class relationships had been fixed. It may seem strange to think of the samurai still wearing two swords and living and behaving much as they did in the thirteenth century until several years after our Civil War, but it is also true that there were still remnants of chivalry and its code in that war, too, particularly in the South. Much of the Southern cavalry was drawn from the landed gentry, some troops still carried lances, and almost all of them—at least at the beginning of the war—thought of themselves as knights without armor and behaved with knightly courtesy towards their foes.

The first actual attempt to set down a code of behavior for the samurai was the *Azuma Kagami* or "Mirror of the East" which was written about 1270. It was principally history, covering events up to the Mongol invasions, but it also listed some basic principles for the samurai to follow such as:

"The warrior does not ask for favors from his lord. He counts on his leadership and protection, but makes no conditions for the service he owes him. Their relationship is based entirely on the samurai's loyalty. The samurai does not question the commands of his lord, but obeys them regardless of life, family, or personal interests. In defeat, he must remember what he owes his lord for past favors and must be ready to die in the cause of his lord, his lord's family or clan."

The word most often associated with the code of the samurai is *Bushido,* pronounced Bóoshi-dóh and meaning Way of the Warrior. The word *Bushido* first appears in the latter half of the sixteenth century, and the first recorded use of it is shortly after this in a handbook for young samurai written by Daidoji Yusan and called *The Beginner's Book of Bushido*. A section describes what a samurai's attitude towards death should be:

"If the samurai determines simply to live for today with no thought for tomorrow, so that when he stands before his lord to receive his commands he thinks of it as his last appearance before him, and when he looks at his family he feels he will never see them again, then he will be sincere about his duty and have no difficulty in following the path of loyalty.

"But if he does not keep death in mind, he will be careless and liable to be indiscreet and offend others. To forget death may lead to self-indulgence, the taking of too much food and wine. But those who keep the thought of death constantly before them remain strong and healthy. If you look death in the face, you will have little attachment to material things and no grasping or covetous qualities."

The book then goes on to list the duties and obligations of the samurai, outlining what his education and training should consist of, the books he should read, and the weapons he should be able to handle. It also specifies his dress and food, both of which should be simple, and sets forth points of etiquette which he should observe. For instance:

"When he is lying down, his feet must never point

towards his lord. During archery practice, he must never shoot arrows in a direction where he knows his lord to be, nor permit a sword, spear, or halberd to point towards his lord. If he hears talk about his lord or even hears his name mentioned when he is lying down, he must immediately sit up and assume a respectful attitude."

While there were many books written about Bushido from the sixteenth through the early part of the twentieth century, its greatest strength came from unwritten traditions that developed. In his autobiography, written about 1716, Arai Hakuseki tells a story about his father who, as a young man, was ordered to guard three samurai who had been charged with murder. He insisted that their swords be returned to them. Then, wrapping his own sword in cloth, he said to them, "If you decide to escape, please cut off my head and take it with you since I cannot fight three men."

Completely defenseless, he ate and slept with them for ten days. At the end of that time they were acquitted. They then told him that at first they had agreed to attack him at the first possible opportunity, three unarmed men against a man who was armed. However, when he returned their swords to them and rendered his own useless, they changed their minds.

"It was far better for us to stand trial and even to die," they said, "than for three armed men to attack one man who was not armed."

The essence of the samurai code is given in one short sentence in Daidoji Yusan's book which states: "In Bushido, three qualities are essential: Loyalty, Right Conduct, and Bravery." Of these, loyalty—even unto death—was the most important. Japanese history is full of examples of samurai who begged to be permitted to take their lord's place during a retreat, put on his armor, and died fighting so that he could escape. One incident of a different type, but calling for the same qualities, took place during the time of Oda Nobunaga.

Okudaira Nobumasa was besieged in a castle by Takeda Katsuyori, and the defenders were running out of food. Torii Suneyemon offered to try and get through the enemy lines and ask Tokugawa Ieyasu for help. He did get through the enemy lines and, when he reached Ieyasu's camp, he was told that Ieyasu was starting immediately to lift the siege. Torii was commended for his bravery and told to remain in the camp, but he refused, starting back to the castle to bring the news to the starving defenders. He was captured by Takedo Katsuyori's forces, however, and offered his life and a handsome reward if he would say that he had not been able to get through and that his lord had better surrender. A note was shot into the castle on an arrow, summoning the defenders to the walls, and Torii was tied to a cross set up near the main gate.

"Speak!" he was told.

With the points of several spears pressing against his chest, he shouted, "You will be relieved in less than three days! Stand fast!"

He died, but foe as well as friend honored his memory.

It was this training from infancy to face death that made it possible for a samurai to face even as difficult and painful a death as *seppuku* with quiet composure. And even this particular form of ceremonial suicide had its roots in the warrior's code. For the Japanese believed, as the ancient Greeks did, that the soul was to be found in the abdomen. So when a samurai disembowelled himself in the accepted manner, he was saying, "I show you my soul. You can see for yourself whether it is clean or not."

The samurai, however, was often called on to sacrifice far more than his own life for his honor or his lord. A warrior might substitute his own son for that of his lord and rejoice if the death of his own child helped preserve that of his lord's.

What was lacking in the military life as actually practiced were certain moral principles, the most important of which—at least to a ruling class that was trying to maintain itself in power—was loyalty. That was why there was such accent on this particular quality in all the military codes, written and unwritten.

It is possible to play up the courage and self-sacrifice of the samurai and completely ignore the treachery and self-seeking that runs like a dark thread through Japanese history. And this is what has often been done. But as one example among an infinite number of such incidents, there is the manner in which Ashikaga Takauji came into power. He was sent from Kamakura by the Hojo regent to put down an imperial uprising in Kyoto early in the fourteenth century. Before he left, the regent had him renew his loyalty, pledging himself with written, sacred, and unbreakable oaths. Upon reaching Kyoto, Takauji immediately joined forces with the emperor and marched back to Kamakura, destroying it and the house to which he had just pledged his allegiance.

This is not to say that there were no virtues in the military code and that it did not make contributions to Japanese culture. But to pretend that it was always observed in all its details is as naive as it is to believe that there were no false or renegade knights in Europe during the Age of Chivalry or that the precepts of Christianity have always been followed in the West.

By the middle of the seventeenth century a middle class began to develop in Japan as it had developed earlier in Europe. The growing wealth of the townspeople began to put a strain on the feudal system, bringing the old and the new into conflict.

There was no real place for the samurai in the new social structure. A large military class can be a nuisance in times of peace, and Japan had been at peace for a long time. With no chance to practise the profession for which they had been trained, the samurai became unruly, threatening the peace with their brawling and blood-feuds; and the whole concept of Bushido became artificial, abstract, and philosophical rather than the living reality it had once been. But, because the Shogunate needed the support of the military class to remain in power, it had to give at least lip service to ancient custom.

This conflict between the old and the new, the contradictions between a feudal code of honor and a growing bureaucracy whose ideals and aspirations were generally middle-class, is dramatized in the story of the Forty Seven Ronin. Its mixture of courage and cruelty, loyalty and treachery, passion and cold calculation has moved and inspired the Japanese ever since the incident occurred.

In the year 1701, as was his custom every spring, the emperor sent two emissaries to make a ceremonial call on the Shogun. The purpose of this was to demonstrate to the country the cordial relations that existed between the Imperial Throne and the Shogunate. Each year the Shogun appointed two daimyo to receive the imperial officials. In 1701 the daimyo appointed were Asano Takumi no Kami and Kamei Sama. Since the ceremonies involved in any contact with a representative of the Imperial Throne were extremely elaborate, both daimyo required instruction in court etiquette. This instruction was to be given to them by Kira Kotsuke no Suke, master of ceremonies at the Shogun's court. This was exactly the kind of occasion that Kira lived for. It not only made him important, but it was very profitable; for the daimyo he instructed, anxious for his good will, almost invariably gave him very expensive gifts. Though Kamei Sama was not very rich, his steward wisely gave Kira the expected gifts and Kira rubbed his hands, sure that he would get even more lavish ones from the far richer Asano. But Asano's steward and councilor, Oishi Kuranosuke, had not come to Yedo, the seat of the Shogun with his lord, and Asano—possibly because he did not believe it was morally right to give gifts to an official who was only doing his job—did not offer Kira anything.

Kira was furious and made things very difficult for Asano, not only refusing to teach him the proper ceremonial behavior, but constantly insulting him. The ceremonies were supposed to last for three days. By watching Kamei Sama, who had been carefully coached by Kira, Asano was able to get through the first two. But by the morning of the third day his nerves were strained to the breaking point. Just as the morning ceremonies were about to begin, Kira said to him, "The ribbon of my sock has come undone. Tie it up for me."

Burning with rage, Asano still felt it was his duty to obey; and he knelt and tied up the ribbon of the sock. But when he had done so, Kira pulled away from him and said, "How clumsy you are! Why, you can't even tie a ribbon properly. Anyone can see that you're a country boor and that you know nothing of court manners!"

Asano could stand no more. Whipping out his short sword, he slashed at Kira, but Kira's court cap deflected the blow and he only wounded him slightly. Asano cut again, but Kira was running now, and again he was only wounded. Then armed attendants seized Asano.

The penalty for drawing a sword in the palace of the Shogun was death; and Asano's punishment was not only prompt, but even more severe than might have been expected. For though the Shogun's councilors advised an investigation, aware that Kira had provoked the assault and suspecting the reason for it, the Shogun overruled them. He not only ordered Asano to kill himself, but confiscated his castle and all his holdings. That night, in the garden of a nearby mansion, Asano died by his own hand; bravely as a samurai should die, but also bitterly, knowing that his family was now ruined and penniless.

Some four days later the news of what had happened came to Oishi Kuranosuke, Asano's steward, at Asano's castle at Ako. Oishi immediately called together Asano's three hundred retainers, now masterless men or ronin. Their first task, he told them, was to try and have the fief restored to Asano's younger brother, now the head of the family. At the same time they should fight to the end to hold the castle, refuse to surrender it to the Shogun. There was considerable disagreement about this, many of the retainers feeling that if they fought it would only make things worse for everyone concerned.

When, under orders from the Shogun, the neighboring daimyo began mobilizing to take the castle by force, Oishi called another conference. This time, out of the three hundred retainers, only sixty-one appeared. The rest had decided that they did not wish to fight in what was obviously a lost cause. Now Oishi told the loyal retainers the truth. He agreed that it would be useless to try and hold the castle against the armed might of the Shogunate. What he had been trying to do was to weed out the faint-hearted. This he had succeeded in doing, for those who remained were true samurai. It was important, he told them, to try and have the castle and other holdings restored to the Asano family, and this they would attempt to do. But there was something else that was just as important. Kira had destroyed their master as surely as if he had done it with a sword. They must take vengeance on him. With a cheer, the faithful retainers pledged themselves to do so.

What Oishi and his companions had sworn to accomplish was not only difficult and complicated, but extremely dangerous. The vendetta or blood-feud was sanctioned by custom and by law, but there was a regular procedure for it. Anyone who intended to take such vengeance had to give notice of it in writing to the local authorities, who then forwarded it to the central government. This vengeance was considered the right and duty of a man's nearest relatives or retainers under the Confucian doctrine that a man could not live under the same heaven as the murderer of his father or his lord. But Asano's retainers could not give such notice because Kira was a high official with powerful friends and, if he were warned, he would be so well guarded that they would never have a chance to get near him. Therefore they would have to act without giving notice, that is, secretly and illegally.

The first thing they would have to do was convince Kira that he had nothing to fear from them. This was easier to do than it would have been a century or so before, since the times had changed considerably. There had been no warfare for almost a hundred years. The country's wealth was moving from the purses of the feudal lords to those of the merchants in the towns. The national mood was materialistic and, not merely gay, but licentious. Even the samurai were more interested in pleasure-seeking than in the obligations and simplicity of their historic code.

Having settled the affairs of the Asano family and entered a plea for the return of the estate to Asano's brother, Oishi moved to a house on the outskirts of Kyoto with his wife and children. The rest of the faithful retainers scattered, many of them settling in Yedo where they could keep watch on Kira. As ronin, masterless men without any status to protect, they all tried to lose their identity, disguising themselves as merchants or craftsmen.

Oishi, of course, was too well-known to do this; but when he was offered employment by other feudal lords, he refused, claiming he had retired. Kira, however, was still suspicious. He had resigned his post at court, strengthened his mansion at Yedo until it was virtually a fortress, and enlisted the aid of his wife's family to defend him; but he was still uneasy. He kept sending spies to watch Oishi and make sure he was as harmless as he seemed.

To throw Kira further off guard, Oishi now began to live a life that caused anguish to those who had respected him before. He plunged into a life of complete dissipation. One day he staggered out of a wine shop so drunk that he could not get home, but fell down and went to sleep in the street, much to the amusement of the onlookers. One of these was a samurai from Satsuma who recognized him and said, "Isn't this Oishi Kuranosuke who was once steward of Lord Asano and whom everyone once admired? Look at him now. Instead of avenging his lord, he lies here like a common drunkard. I spit on him!" And he not only spat on him, but spurned him with his sandal.

Finally, even Oishi's patient and understanding wife could endure his behavior no longer and protested about it. Flying into a rage, or appearing to, Oishi promptly divorced her and sent her and his three youngest children back to her father, keeping his oldest son, Chikara, with him. Looking back, it now seems obvious that he divorced her and sent her and his children away to protect them from the consequences of his actions.

With his wife gone, Oishi's life became even more dissolute. This period has often been pictured as one of great self-sacrifice for Oishi, but this is very doubtful. The times were generally pleasure-seeking and sensual, and he was a man of his times. He knew he probably had very little longer to live, was determined to make the most of it, and did. He undoubtedly enjoyed himself thoroughly, especially since he could tell himself that what he was doing was in the best possible cause.

There were repercussions, of course. If his conduct fooled Kira into thinking that he had nothing to fear from such a depraved fellow, it also disgusted some of his former companions and they gave up all thought of vengeance. One of them even killed himself in despair and disappointment.

In July, about a year and a half after Asano's death, word was received that the Shogunate had decided that the Asano estates would not be returned to the family. There was no longer any reason for the faithful retainers to hold back from revenge. At the same time, Oishi also heard a rumor that Kira was planning to leave Yedo and seek refuge in the castle of his wife's family, deep in the mountains. If he did this, the task of the ronin would become far more difficult, probably impossible. Therefore they would have to move fast.

Oishi sent a message to all the still loyal ronin saying he would be in Yedo early in November and telling them to meet him there. At the end of the first week in November, he arrived at an inn in Yedo. His son, Chikara, was already there posing as a young merchant, and Oishi claimed to be his uncle and guardian. The other members of the faithful band were scattered about the city in disguise, and under assumed names, keeping watch on Kira.

They learned that Kira was to give a tea ceremony on the afternoon of the fourteenth and would probably be home that night. They decided to make their attack then. Of the original three hundred retainers, sixty-one had pledged themselves to vengeance; but some of these had dropped out, and Oishi had weeded out others because he did not feel he could trust them. When they gathered at about midnight to carry out their oath, there were only forty-seven.

They were all dressed in new clothing, for what they were doing was in the nature of a rite. Over their coats of mail they wore black silk kimonos, trouser-like *hakama,* and black and white mantles with hoods

that covered their helmets. It had snowed that day, and it was bitter cold as they set out at two in the morning, marching through the deserted streets toward Kira's mansion.

When they reached it, they divided into two parties. One, led by Chikara, went around to the rear gate, prepared to break it down. Oishi led the other party. They scaled the main gate with ladders, overpowered the guards, and gave the signal. Chikara's party broke in by the rear gate and joined them. Before they began their attack on the house itself, Oishi stationed men about the courtyard to keep any of Kira's retainers from going to get help. He also sent a messenger to the nearby houses to reassure Kira's neighbors, and tell them that they were not thieves but men carrying out a vendetta. Since Kira was not particularly well-liked by his neighbors, none of them even tried to come to his aid.

Now Oishi gave the signal for the attack. Some ten of Kira's retainers, roused by the noise, were waiting in the front room, prepared to defend their master. They were joined by additional men from the barracks. The battle began, swords flashing in the lantern light. The fighting was savage while it lasted, but it did not last long. Some of Kira's men fought to the end and were killed, but others—including Kira's son—dropped their swords and fled. Though some of the ronin were wounded, none of them was killed. They broke into Kira's chamber. His bed was still warm, but he was not in it. They searched the house, but could not find him. They questioned the terrified women and servants, but none of them knew where he was.

An hour went by, and it began to look as if Kira had escaped them after all. Then one of the ronin found an old hut in the back yard in which charcoal was stored. When he opened the door, two men came out fighting. He engaged them and called for help. Other ronin ran up, found a third man in the hut, and wounded him with a spear thrust. When he came out with a short sword in his hand, he was killed with another spear thrust. A lantern was brought out, and the ronin sighed with relief. It was Kira. Their vengeance had been accomplished.

Cutting off Kira's head and wrapping it in his kimono, they posted a statement on the main gate of the house, explaining who they were, what they had done, and why. Then they set off, forty-seven weary and blood-stained men, for the temple of Sengakuji where their lord was buried. It was broad daylight, about eight in the morning, when they reached the temple. They washed Kira's head at a nearby well and placed it before Asano's tomb. Then each in turn kneeled at the tomb, burned incense, and prayed. When the ceremony was over, the abbot invited them into the temple and gave them food.

After they had eaten, two of the group were sent to the Shogun's court to make a formal report of their action. They remained at the temple all that day and that night. The next day they were divided into four groups and were put in the custody of four different daimyo, each of whom made a point of showing how much he honored and respected his prisoners.

The Shogun and his council now began to consider the case. It wasn't an easy one to decide because there were many factors involved. What they had done was not only proper but praiseworthy according to the feudal code. At the same time, even forgetting that they had not given notice of their vendetta, what they had done was, in a sense, a protest against the Shogun's decision concerning Asano. In addition, if they were pardoned, it might encourage others to take the law into their own hands and resort to violence.

Most of the major government officials were called in to study the problem. Scholars wrote briefs on it, examining the moral issues that were at stake. The debate lasted for three months, with the whole country involved and taking part in it privately. But though the Shogun himself appears to have wished to pardon the ronin, the final decision went against them. On a gray morning early in February, a representative of the Shogunate told them what their sentence was; and at dusk each carried out that sentence himself; all wore white garments and kneeled on reversed mats, and all died at the same time in the four separate mansions where they had been quartered.

The people of Japan were outraged. Considering the gallant forty-seven to be heroes, and ignoring the political and social questions involved, they had been convinced that the men would be pardoned and were furious when they were not. All forty-seven of the ronin were buried at the temple of Sengakuji in front of the tomb of their master. Not two weeks after their death, the first dramatization of their story appeared on the Yedo stage. Generally called *Chushingura,* it has been produced hundreds of times since, and dozens of film versions of it have been made.

But the story is not quite ended. Next to the tombs of the forty-seven ronin at the temple of Sengakuji is a forty-eighth tomb. When word of their deed and their deaths became known, people came from all parts of Japan to pray at their graves. Among them was the samurai from Satsuma who had been incensed at Oishi's behavior in Kyoto. Prostrating himself before Oishi's tomb, he said, "When I saw you lying drunk in the gutter in Kyoto, I did not realize what you were planning to do, and thinking you a faithless man and no samurai, I spat upon you and spurned you with my foot. I have now come here to ask your pardon and offer atonement for that insult."

Tucking up his robe, he drew his dagger and killed himself before Oishi's tomb. His tomb is the forty-eighth in the enclosure; for the understanding abbot of the temple had him buried next to the Forty-Seven Ronin, linking him with them in death as he had already linked himself to them in the observance of the feudal code.

While Bushido was an expression of the traditions of the military class, it could not help but have an effect on the other classes. After all, from the earliest times Japan's heroes had been members of the warrior class. The people's appreciation of the basic principles of the samurai code is evident in their reaction to the deaths of the Forty Seven Ronin.

But times were changing and, admirable as some of the precepts of Bushido were, there are some pressures which principles cannot withstand. The samurai faced the same contradictions that the Shogunate faced in trying to decide the fate of Asano's faithful retainers. A military class cannot exist indefinitely without a state of war; and, while it was possible for the samurai to despise wealth and material things when their needs were taken care of by their feudal lords, it became impossible when the daimyo became impoverished and could no longer support them.

IV

*The Treasures
and the
Modern World*

明治維新
文明開化

12

The End of the Samurai

FIVE YEARS after the Civil War in the United States was over, Japan was still a feudal state. While the golden spike was being driven near Ogden, Utah, signalling the fact that our east and west coasts were linked by rail, members of a hereditary warrior class walked through the streets of Yedo and Kyoto with two swords thrust through their sashes. However, their long day was coming to an end.

Japan had been in serious economic difficulties through most of the eighteenth century, and these problems became even more acute in the early part of the nineteenth century. The chief cause of these difficulties was the fact that her economy was based on the farm. Most of the burden of supporting the unwieldy state structure rested on the shoulders of the poor farmer. The life of the peasant, difficult at the best of times, was made almost unbearable at this time by the fluctuating price of rice and by the rising standard of living among almost all the other classes. Though forbidden to do so by law, the farmers began to leave the land. The production of rice fell, and the whole economy suffered.

After the peasants, the class that suffered most from the economic crisis was the samurai. The income of the feudal lords and the amount that they paid to their retainers was expressed in quantities of rice. When, in spite of constant increases in taxes, the income of the daimyo fell, they reduced the amounts paid to their retainers and times became harder and harder for the samurai.

At about the same time, another custom began to become quite common. When a samurai became hard pressed financially, he would adopt the son of a rich commoner as his heir in exchange for a good sum of money. This meant that the samurai could no longer afford to despise all the other classes and pride themselves on the purity of their blood and the dignity of their family name. By the end of the Tokugawa regime it was quite usual and accepted for a commoner to purchase the rank of samurai, something that would have been impossible in earlier times.

Meanwhile pressure of another sort was being exerted on Japan. Since 1639, all foreign powers but the Dutch had been barred from Japan; and the Dutch were limited to trading at a tiny island in the harbor of Nagasaki. But trade had become too important for the European powers and the United States to permit this policy of exclusion to continue. The British, the French, and the Russians all made attempts during the early part of the nineteenth century to get Japan to change this policy, but without success.

In July, 1853, when the British, French, and Russians were all involved in the Crimean War, Commodore Matthew C. Perry sailed into Uraga Bay outside of Yedo with four United States gunboats. He insisted on seeing a suitable representative of the Shogun to whom he could deliver a letter from President Fillmore. With gunboats at its doorstep, and both its finances and coastal defenses very weak, the Shogunate could not send Perry away as it had sent away representatives of the other foreign powers. The governor of Uraga was forced to accept the letter in which President Fillmore requested friendship, commerce, and arrangements to supply coal and provisions to American ships.

Having delivered the letter, Perry sailed away, stating that he would be returning for an answer. Some seven months later, in February, 1854, he returned with ten ships instead of four. Though there were many in Japan who wanted to fight, the Shogunate was aware enough of its own weakness and the strength of the foreign powers to know that this was impossible. A treaty of friendship was signed with the United States, and this was followed by other treaties with other foreign powers. In 1858, a trade treaty was signed. The closed door to the outside world was opened. But for the next ten years Japan was torn by conflicting impulses: on the one hand there was a desire to drive out the foreigners and return to old ways, and on the other a desire to learn everything possible from the Western powers.

In 1867, under pressure from a powerful group of daimyo who had long been opposed to the Shoguns, the Shogunate surrendered its authority to the young Emperor Mutsuhito. Thus, for the first time in almost seven hundred years, an emperor became the actual ruler of Japan. A new era, known as the *Meiji,* or Period of Enlightened Government, began.

Since Yedo had been the seat of government for so long under the Shoguns, the young emperor and his advisers now moved there from Kyoto. They changed its name to Tokyo, which means Eastern Capital.

Then, a year later, something very remarkable happened. Though feudalism had begun to decline in the fifteenth century in Europe, it took centuries to abolish it completely. In Japan, where feudalism had lasted for a far longer time, it was abolished almost overnight. In 1868, the seventeen-year-old emperor presented the nobles and daimyo of Japan with the

Charter Oath, which called for a completely new form
of government, including a deliberative assembly. Led
by the daimyo of the southwest, who had originally
supported the emperor, the entire class of feudal lords
voluntarily surrendered the lands and privileges they
had held for a thousand years, turning over all their
estates to the emperor.

The daimyo were granted pensions of one-tenth
the revenue of the estates they had given up. Pensions
were also granted to the samurai—for a time, at
least—to take the place of the allowance in rice they
had formerly received from their feudal lords. After
a few years, however, even this pension was stopped,
and the samurai had to look after themselves. Some
of them, badly handicapped by their attitude towards
money and commerce, tried to go into business and
failed miserably. Others, better equipped because they
had handled the finances of their feudal lords, became
very successful in banking and industry or rose to
posts of importance in the government.

From the time when foreigners first began appearing in Japan, there had been numerous occasions
when they had been attacked and either wounded or
killed by samurai or ronin who bitterly resented all
that they stood for. In his *Tales of Old Japan,* published in 1871, Lord Redesdale wrote that though the
statesman who passed a law forbidding the samurai
to wear their swords would deserve the praise of all
Japan, his life would not be worth much. Five years
later, in 1876, such a law was passed, and the Japanese astonished even those who knew them best.
Quietly, without violence or protest, the military class
that had transferred its loyalty from individual feudal
lords to the emperor and the country as a whole, gave

up the sign of its rank as it had given up its privileges. Some of them put their swords in safe and honored places in their homes, keeping them as family heirlooms. But many others were in such financial difficulties that they sold theirs, and noble blades became a drug on the market. The Age of the Samurai was over.

Though many of the samurai went into industry and government, others, of course, went into the armed forces. These were now, for the first time in many hundreds of years, conscripted from the nation as a whole. The modern world had its first opportunity to judge the mettle of the Japanese fighting man in 1894 during Japan's brief war with China. This campaign was an unbroken series of victories for the Japanese, though China put almost a million men in the field.

The West had another opportunity to observe the men from Nippon in action during the Russo-Japanese War in 1904. It was during the fiercely contested and costly siege of Port Arthur that Take Hirose, one of the heroes of the siege, wrote:

> As infinite as the dome of heaven above us
> Is the debt we owe our emperor;
> Immeasurable as the deep sea below us
> Is the debt we owe our country.
> The time has come for us to pay our debts.

And when General Nogi was informed that his son had been killed, he said quietly, "It is an honor that the Nation has accepted this humble sacrifice."

It was obvious that though the samurai had ceased to exist as a class, their traditions and the code by which they had lived was still very much alive.

During World War I, Japan joined the Allies, though she did not send troops to Europe, and by 1918 she had taken her place among the world powers. In fifty years she had transformed herself from a bankrupt feudal state into a modern nation almost twice her original size. As a result of the Sino-Japanese and Russo-Japanese Wars and her participation in World War I, she had annexed Korea, acquired Formosa, the Pescadores, the southern half of the island of Sakhalin, and a mandate over the Caroline, Marshall, and Mariana Islands.

In 1931, with military extremists in control of her government, Japan began a long war of expansion in China. Turning her face from the West, which had frowned on her attack on China, the whole nation was put on a war footing. Again, echoes from the past—from the precepts of the old samurai code—were heard in phrases like: "The highest hope of a member of our race is to die for the emperor." and "Duty is weightier than a mountain; death lighter than a feather."

In 1939, when Japan had taken over almost a third of China, the United States nullified its commercial treaty with her, cutting off most of the raw materials she needed for her industries. When World War II broke out, Japan moved into Indo-China. She was now within striking distance of the British bases in Malaya and the American base in the Philippines. On December 7, 1941, she struck Pearl Harbor and elsewhere; and, as a partner of Hitler and the Axis powers, she began undeclared war against the West.

There is no need to recount the progress of the war in detail. After early victories, Japan suffered a series of defeats: at Midway, Guadalcanal, and the Coral Seas. The military rulers of Japan began putting more and more accent on what were to them the most useful elements of the old samurai code: on the loyalty required of a fighting man, which must be unquestioning, and on his willingness to die for his emperor and his country. These were reflected in *banzai* attacks when Japanese troops, knowing their situation was hopeless and often led by officers wielding samurai swords, charged superior forces determined to kill as many of the enemy as possible before they were killed themselves. Even more graphic examples were the suicide attacks launched during the latter part of the war by pilots who attempted to sink American ships by diving their bomb-laden planes into them. To give the doomed pilots a sense of history, these attacks were called *kamikaze* after the Divine Wind that had saved Japan from the Mongol invaders almost seven hundred years before.

But Japan was no match for the angry, mobilized strength of the West, and even the fury of the original Divine Wind could not begin to be compared with the devastating effect of splitting atoms.

In 1945, with much of Tokyo destroyed by conventional bombs, and with Hiroshima and Nagasaki smouldering in ruins from the searing blast of atom bombs, the Japanese people, for the first time, heard their emperor's voice. It went out over the Japanese radio to even the smallest and most remote villages, saying, "We have resolved to pave the way for a peace for all the generations to come by enduring the unendurable and suffering what is insufferable."

There was a good deal of concern in the West about how the Japanese would react to their defeat and how they would behave toward their conquerors. In all their long history they had never been occupied by another power. But again they astonished the world. For they greeted the occupying forces with almost no anger or bitterness, showing them warm courtesy and cooperating with them in a way that the Americans found almost unbelievable.

There were several reasons for this. In the first place, for some decades the military rulers of Japan had been trying to extend their sway by force of arms. The Japanese people may well have felt that it was only just for those who had attempted to rule by the sword to be themselves ruled by another's sword.

But there was another reason, one that stemmed from Japan's long history and was related to the personality of the man who headed the occupation forces. From the end of the twelfth century to almost the end of the nineteenth, although there was always an emperor on the throne, the actual power was in the hands of a Shogun. And General Douglas MacArthur, Supreme Commander for the Allied Powers, must have appeared to them as another such figure: a professional soldier, authoritative, austere and remote, and exactly the kind of man who should be helping to guide them in the troubled postwar period.

Called Makkasa Gensui—Commander-in-Chief MacArthur–by the Japanese, the way in which he was accepted by them is demonstrated by a well-known story. An American asked a Japanese official what he thought of the general.

"The emperor could not have picked a better man," said the Japanese.

In 1946 a new Japanese constitution was drafted by the occupation officials. It went into effect a year later. In the old constitution the emperor had been described as "combining in Himself the rights of sovereignty." In the new one he was called "the symbol of the State and of the unity of the people, deriving his position from the will of the people with whom resides sovereign power."

But there is another section of the constitution that is even more important. Article 9 reads:

"Aspiring sincerely to an international peace based on justice and order, the Japanese people forever renounce war as a sovereign right of the nation and the threat or use of force as a means of settling international disputes.

"In order to accomplish the aims of the preceding paragraph, land, sea and air forces, as well as other war potential, will never be maintained. The right of belligerency of the state will not be recognized."

When the Japanese people accepted their new constitution, and with it this section and all it implies, they ceased to be—as they had been for some time—the People of the Sword and the Sword alone. They became once more what they had been originally, the People of the Three Treasures. The contrasting qualities that the Three Treasures represent, were once again in balance. The Sword became again what it once had been, not a weapon, but a symbol of self-restraint and of their ability to blend together perfectly the natural elements of which it was forged. The face they saw when they looked in the Sacred Mirror was a new and shining one; and—inspired by the Jewel, the emperor whose love of nature was well-known, could write in his New Year's poem for the year 1960:

This is my wish:
That the rays of the rising sun
May impartially light the corners of the world.

Notes on Japanese Names
and Pronunciation

THE Japanese always put the surname or family name first and follow it with the given name. This order is followed in this book. Thus the name of Yoritomo, one of the most famous members of the Minamoto family, is given as Minamoto Yoritomo. However, in the interests of brevity and simplicity and following the Japanese practice when an individual's family has been clearly identified, the family name is dropped. Thus, for the most part, Minamoto Yoshitsune is referred to merely as Yoshitsune.

The pronounciation of Japanese words and names is simple and regular. The consonants are pronounced as in English—except that the *g* is always hard—and the vowels as in Italian, except shorter. There are no silent letters, and all syllables are given equal accent. Thus *Ise* is pronounced *Ee-say* and *katana, ka-ta-na.*

Major Periods of Japanese History

THE major periods of Japanese history are generally divided as follows:

ARCHAIC PERIOD *(Before 552 A.D.).* Primitive people live on the islands. Mongol people from the Asiatic mainland migrate to Japan and settle there. The country becomes partially unified around the beginning of the fourth century.

ASUKA PERIOD *(552–710).* So called because the court was located at a place of that name near Nara in Yamato Province. Buddhism is introduced from China and has a decided influence on the arts. Prince Shotoku draws up the first major code of laws. While, according to art historians, the Asuka Period only lasted until 645 A.D. and was followed by the Hakuho Period, political historians generally call the entire period the Asuka.

NARA PERIOD *(710–794).* The first permanent capital is built at Nara and further influences Japanese art. Buddhism wins wide acceptance, and Japanese culture comes under Chinese influence.

HEIAN PERIOD *(794–1185).* A new capital called Heian-kyo (now Kyoto) is built. Native art and literature flourish and reach a high state of development. The Fujiwara family becomes more powerful than the emperor.

KAMAKURA PERIOD *(1185–1333).* The first true Shogunate established at Kamakura by Minamoto Yoritomo. It becomes the center of government though the imperial court remains at Kyoto. Zen Buddhism is adopted by the samurai. The Mongols attempt to invade Japan.

ASHIKAGA AND MUROMACHI PERIODS *(1333–1573).* The Ashikaga Shogunate established by Ashikaga Takauji. The Shogunate moves to the Muromachi quarter of Kyoto in 1392 and from then on the period is known by that name. The *Nō* drama and the tea ceremony become popular. The Portuguese arrive and introduce Christianity.

THE PERIOD OF THE WARRING PROVINCES OR THE AZUCHI-MOMOYAMA PERIOD *(1573–1603).* Japanese historians call this the Period of the Country at War (Sengoku Jidai). But the art historians call it the Azuchi-Momoyama Period after Nobunaga's castle at Azuchi and a palace built by Hideyoshi at Momoyama. A period of civil war during which the country is unified by Hideyoshi. It ends when he is succeeded by Tokugawa Ieyasu.

TOKUGAWA OR YEDO PERIOD *(1603–1868).* Tokugawa Ieyasu moves the capital from Kyoto to Yedo so the period is known by both names. A period of peace with a strong central government. Christianity is suppressed. Japan's isolation ends with the arrival of Perry in 1853.

MEIJI PERIOD *(1868–1912).* The emperor returns to power and his reign is known as the Meiji or Period of Enlightened Government. Feudalism ends, and the samurai cease to exist as a class. A period of governmental reform in which Western patterns are adopted. Japan begins her territorial expansion, defeats China and Russia, and becomes a world power.

TAISHO PERIOD *(1912–1926).* Named after the emperor who ruled during this time. Japan takes part in World War I, acquires new territory.

SHOWA PERIOD *(1926–).* Named after the reign of the Emperor Hirohito. Continuation of Japan's expansionist policy involves her in World War II. Japan surrenders and is occupied. Period of occupation ends and Japanese independence is restored with the signing of the San Francisco Treaty in 1952.

Further Reading

THE serious student of Japan cannot do better than the works of Sir George B. Sansom. His *Japan: A Short Cultural History* (Appleton-Century-Crofts, Revised Edition, 1962) covers both the political and cultural history of Japan from the earliest times to the Meiji Period. His three volume *History of Japan* (Stanford University Press, 1958: 1961; third volume to come) is even more detailed and comprehensive.

The Pageant of Japanese History by Marion Dilts (David McKay, Revised, 1961) is a simple book for younger readers and covers Japanese history and culture from their beginnings to the present day. It is a very useful introductory book.

Dr. Daisetz Suzuki is one of the greatest living authorities on Zen Buddhism. Those who are interested in this subject and its influence on Japan will find his *Zen and Japanese Culture* (Pantheon, 1959) fascinating and lucid.

Oliver Statler's *Japanese Inn* (Random House, 1961) is highly recommended for those with a general interest in Japan. It covers many of the main events in Japanese history from the latter part of the sixteenth century to the present day in semi-fictional form and is authoritative, well-written, and profusely illustrated. It is also available in paperback.

Langdon Warner's *Enduring Art of Japan* (Harvard, 1952; Grove Press, 1958) is another well-written, authoritative and profusely illustrated book. In addition to its survey of Japanese art, it has sections on Zen, Japanese gardens, and the tea ceremony.

The anthology, *Japanese Literature*, compiled and edited by Donald Keene, (Grove Press, 1955) is an excellent and comprehensive work for those interested in this aspect of Japanese culture. It contains selections from the earliest Japanese literature to that of the present day.

Ruth Benedict's *Chrysanthemum and the Sword* (Houghton Mifflin Company, 1946) is a fascinating study of the Japanese character and the forces that shaped it by one of our foremost cultural anthropologists.

Index

Robert Newman

is a native New Yorker and has been a writer
for many years. He is the author of two novels,
magazine articles and plays for films, radio and
television. The impetus for this book came from
his active interests in archery, fencing and, of
course, Japan.